The Teen's Guide to Adulting: Social and Self-Organization Skills That Every Young Adult Should Know

Unlock Your Full Potential with Essential Skills in Time Management, Self-Confidence, Money Mastery, Cyber Smarts, Healthy Habits, Career Clarity and Coping Strategies

James Newman

CONTENTS

INTRODUCTION

Before we begin all the life skills development work, let me just tell you how excited I am to have you read this book. It gives me great pleasure to see so many young minds actively searching for useful resources to groom their minds, shape their personalities, and boost their self-esteem. When I was your age, I had no clue as to what to do with my life. It took a series of stupid mistakes and a lot of self-healing for me to learn my lessons the hard way. It is true that during your teenage years, you face an unforeseen mix of problems, confusion, emotional rush, and rapid growth. Those challenges are still the same, but today I see young teens exploring the power of self-awareness, unlocking their confidence, and working on their life skills to prepare well for the challenges ahead. I find that extremely amazing, and you all deserve a pat on the back for beginning this lifelong journey of personal development.

Now, let's get down to the content of this book! Why should you read it? What does it have for you? It is a guide that is going to equip you with all sorts of techniques and methods to deal with the tricky parts of teenage life. Whether you are going through self-esteem issues, relationship troubles, or friendship.

Academic expectations, relationships, peer pressures, and self-discovery—they all make teenage life one big, massive maze, and we often go round and round without knowing how to crack this puzzle and get out of it successfully. A lot of changes occur when we step into the teenage years and feeling overwhelmed amidst all this is only natural. Take the example of our comic teenage characters, for instance! Yes, this book is not all words and lessons; we are going to explore the lives of a group of six amazing teens who, despite their great strengths, are grappling with issues of self-esteem, navigating relationships, managing finances, and much more. Let me introduce you to the protagonists of our comic!

ZARA CARTER: THE BOHEMIAN TRAILBLAZER

ZARA IS ONE WHO EMBRACES HER INDIVIDUALITY, AND YOU CAN SEE THAT THROUGH HER BOHEMIAN-STYLE OUTFITS AND LAYERED JEWELRY. SHE IS FEARLESS AND ENCOURAGES HER FRIENDS TO BE TRUE TO THEMSELVES AND EXPRESS THEIR UNIQUE PERSONALITIES.

MEET SOPHIE TURNER

WITH HER WARM HAZEL EYES AND INFECTIOUS SMILE, SHE IS THE HEART OF THIS GROUP. SHE IS KNOWN FOR HER VINTAGE FASHION SENSE AND POSITIVE ENERGY. SOPHIE CAN EFFORTLESSLY BRING PEOPLE TOGETHER, AND SHE SURE KNOWS HOW TO TURN DULL MOMENTS INTO GREAT ADVENTURES.

THE SKATEBOARDING ENTHUSIAST: OLIVER BAKER

OLIVER IS THE LAID-BACK SKATEBOARD AFICIONADO, WITH HIS SANDY BLOND HAIR AND BLUE EYES. AROUND HIS FRIENDS, OLIVER ALWAYS KEEPS THIS CALM AND CHILL DEMEANOR, BUT DEEP DOWN, HE IS REALLY DRIVEN AND PASSIONATE ABOUT PERFECTING HIS SKATEBOARDING SKILLS.

MAYA JOHNSON: THE REBELLIOUS CREATIVE

MAYA IS THE REBELLIOUS CREATIVE IN THE GROUP. WITH HER PIXIE CUT OF DYED PURPLE HAIR AND GREEN EYES, SHE IS THE EMBODIMENT OF REBELLIOUS CREATIVITY. HER ECLECTIC MIX OF VINTAGE AND PUNK STYLES INSPIRES OTHERS TO BREAK FREE FROM SOCIETAL NORMS AND EXPRESS THEMSELVES FREELY

LIAM THOMPSON: THE EDGY REBEL

YOU KNOW HOW THERE IS ALWAYS THIS ONE EDGY REBEL IN THE GROUP? WELL, THAT IS LIAM! WITH A DARK BROWN MOP OF HAIR AND PIERCING GREEN EYES, HE CARRIES A CASUAL YET EDGY STYLE. DESPITE HIS NO-NONSENSE ATTITUDE, LIAM IS A RELIABLE AND TRUSTWORTHY FRIEND.

AVA PATEL: THE CREATIVE OBSERVER

AVA IS THE CREATIVE HEAD, AND SHE BRINGS A SENSE OF CALM AND CREATIVITY TO THIS GROUP. SHE HAS THIS GREAT ABILITY TO OBSERVE DEEPLY, WHICH IS WHY SHE ALWAYS HAS A FRESH PERSPECTIVE ON LIFE. SHE ENCOURAGES HER FRIENDS TO APPRECIATE THE BEAUTY IN EVERYDAY MOMENTS.

Now that you are familiar with all the characters in this group, it is time to dive headfirst into the exploration of teenage life challenges and then look for their fun, simple, and effective solutions. I know it feels difficult to be a teen, but let me assure you that with a little bit of awareness of yourself and others, you can steer through this phase like a ninja. The skills and techniques you will find in this book will equip you with more than enough confidence to emerge victorious out of this age with lots of golden memories to cherish for years to come.

1

CHAPTER 1:

TECHNIQUES TO BOOST SELF-ESTEEM

The most exhilarating yet challenging chapter of your life is about to begin—the teenage years. When you step into your teenage years you go through this whole identity shift, which makes you feel out of place and often misunderstood.

You know how it feels when you are handed a Rubik's cube and every side is a different mess? That is what your self-esteem is like when facing the challenges of your teenage years. You are figuring out who you are, trying to fit in or stand out, and it is no less than trying to solve a puzzle that keeps changing its own rules. One day, you will feel like the protagonist of your own story, ready to conquer the world. The next day, you are wondering if your wardrobe choice this morning was a cosmic mistake. Yep, that is the teenage magic trick, turning a superhero cape into a security blanket faster than you can say "adolescence."

Amidst all this, the endless comparisons make it even worse. All of your age fellows on social media seem to have their lives together with perfect hair, perfect grades, and perfect morning pancakes. But guess what? Those reels are far from what is real.' Think of it as watching a cooking show where they show the kitchen chaos, the burnt toast, the spilled milk, and everything. You see, life is messy, and everyone's kitchen is filled with chaos.

So those awkward moments—the self-doubt, the feeling of being lost in a sea of expectations—are real. It is the messy kitchen of life, and it is okay. You are not alone in feeling like you are figuring things out as you go. Spoiler alert! Even adults do not have it all together. We are all just pretending we know how to be adults, trust me! We learn, unlearn, and relearn new things as well.

What is most important in this lifelong journey is to stand by your side and believe in yourself or how you see yourself. Your self-esteem and confidence are the two most valuable tools that will help you achieve all your goals and ambitions in life without a shred of self-doubt. There are various amazing techniques that you can employ on a daily basis to counter the external noise of societal expectations, constant comparisons, and unhealthy competition. These confidence-boosting exercises will clear your vision, keep you focused, and elevate your self-esteem.

What Is Self-Perception?

When you look at yourself in the mirror every day, what do you see? A strong, confident teen or someone struggling to accept who they are? The mirror reflects your perception of reality. Our mind creates this mental image of ourselves, which is based on what we think. If you believe you look amazing, you will see the same, or if your mind is loaded with self-doubt, chances are you will focus on your "not-so-visible" flaws. The power of self-perception is so profound that it changes your whole attitude towards life.

The question is: how was this self-perception created in the first place? "Do I have to blame myself for thinking so negatively about myself?" No! While inborn personality traits do influence our perception, they are not the only factors responsible for shaping it. Self-perception is more of an acquired awareness that we develop because of the environment we live in. What would happen if you placed a white-colored page in green-colored water? It will turn green and wet, obviously! That is how our surroundings influence the development of our self-perception; we pick up the colors we live in. In this age, there are various factors at play, such as:

Social Media: Scrolling through your Instagram, Snapchat, and TikTok feeds, you constantly consume content that influences your standards of beauty, success, and accomplishment, and based on those ideals, you start measuring yourself. Sometimes, it messes with your head, making you think everyone's got it together except you. But, to be honest, it is just a slice of reality, not the whole pie.

Peer Pressure: Friends, squads, cliques—they do make your support system, but they can also make you question who you are. When you compare yourself to those close to you, it sparks self-doubt in your mind. But no matter how similar your age group or life situations may be, you and your peers are unique individuals who have their own goals and ambitions to focus on.

Family Ties: Your family makes a big difference. How your parents treat you creates a lasting impact on your mind. Sometimes they get you, sometimes they do not, and their opinions can stick in your head. But always keep in mind that you are your own person, not a mini-me version of your parents or siblings.

Body Changes: Puberty hits everyone like a storm! Your body goes through all these changes, and suddenly you are like, "Whoa, who am I becoming?" Everything shifts along with your emotions. It is normal. Just give yourself time to adjust.

Achievements and Failures: Your wins and losses also shape your self-perception. When you ace a test or win a race, you feel like you are on top of the world. Fail a bit? It stings. However, you should keep in mind that you are not defined by one test or one mistake. It is the whole journey that counts.

Personal Experiences: Life has its way of throwing challenges at us. Relationships, breakups, victories, losses—they all add up to change and mold our self-perception. Your experiences change you, and sometimes they can shake up how you view yourself.

Personality and Interests: Are you the artsy type, a sports fanatic, a science nerd, or a mix of everything? Your interests and personality are a huge part of your self-perception. Accept what makes you who you are.

Self-Perception: Affecting Your Confidence

Do you know that our self-perception often lies to us? Yes! Self-perception is not always right; it can be distorted because of the voices we hear every day. Those confidence-shattering doubts and opinions we hear from people lead to the development of negative self-perception. Whereas, when we see ourselves achieving success and garnering appreciation and appraisal from others, we develop a positive self-perception. This positivity instills confidence and boosts self-esteem.

Can self-esteem change over time?

Yes! Self-esteem does not remain the same throughout our lives. The better you get to know yourself the more confident you become. You start believing in what you have in yourself, instead of listening to the opinions of others. Depending on the conditions we create for ourselves and the influences we allow in our lives, our self-esteem can be boosted. Teenage is the perfect time to give yourself that boost of confidence. It is the beginning of your adulthood, and if you start changing your perception of yourself and practice confidence-boosting exercises, they are going to turn you into a secure and strong adult.

What are your strengths and areas for growth?

Everyone's personality has a mix of strengths and weaknesses; some of you do well in sports but face trouble in class tests, while others might get good grades but can't really socialize well. We are all unique in our own ways. Sure, some traits of our personalities feel like they are holding us back, but seeing them as areas of growth can create space for self-grooming. The idea is to use our strengths to our advantage. Think about it! What are you really good at? It could be playing a sport, drawing, helping others, or even making people laugh. These are your strengths. What makes you, YOU? Your personality, quirks, and what you care about are unique qualities. They make you stand out; you have to embrace them with open arms while ignoring what other people think of you.

Strengths are your superpowers, and weaknesses are your kryptonite. Both of them help you understand yourself better. If you know you are really good at playing guitar but bad at handling a flute, then you would definitely join a band as a guitarist, right? So, understanding your superpowers and kryptonite helps you make the right decisions at the right time. When you know that you are really good at something and believe in your ability, you tell yourself, "Hey! You have got this!" and that is the confidence you need to succeed at things you are good at. But using our superpowers is not the only way to succeed; embracing our weaknesses is also the way to go! How? Well, let me give you an example here! When I was in high school, I had a huge stage fright. I dreaded going onto the stage and performing in front of all my schoolfellows. This was the one weakness that was keeping me from playing piano at music shows, even though I was good at it. I used to think that I would never be able to perform on stage. Even though I had this great passion for sharing my talent with others, my fear of the stage was getting in the way of that. To let my talent shine, I had to overcome my weakness, and when I eventually did that, the rest became easy!

Let's level up!

Imagine you have a strong left hand and a weak right hand. If you keep using your left hand for all the work and ignore the right one because of its weakness, you will end up hurting your back because of the imbalance. This can change by putting your right hand to use, doing some exercises, and gradually making it strong enough to do some basic work. This is how the balance of strengths and weaknesses turns out to be. You have to put your strengths to use, but do this without overshadowing or forgetting about your weaknesses. To level up your confidence game:

1. First, power up your strengths by doing more of what you are good at. If you love art, draw every day. If you are great at playing music, do that!

2. Work on your weaknesses and turn them into strengths. If you are not good at something, practice and learn.

3. Use the power of teaming. There is nothing wrong with collaborating with others. If you are weak in one area, team up with a friend who is an expert in that area. Friends can cover each other's backs.

Love Yourself Unconditionally

Let me ask you a question! Who knows you better than anyone else in the world? Does any particular name come to mind? It is YOU! The longest period of time you spend with anyone is with yourself, and if that inner voice in your head kept saying mean things about you, how would that feel? It is quite draining. With self-compassion, you extend the same kindness to yourself as you would to a friend. Think about it: when you are not convinced yourself that you are capable, confident, and strong, how can you make the world see otherwise? Before anyone else believes in us, it is extremely important for us to believe in ourselves. When you love yourself and appreciate who you are, others will do the same! Self-compassion and acceptance are your ways of telling people, "This is me! This is what I deserve, and this is what I do." Now, I do understand that it is difficult to love yourself when you are facing some failures in life and having trouble understanding your own emotions and feelings while navigating the challenges of the teenage years, but it is possible to see past our mistakes and shortcomings and love ourselves unconditionally. This will take your self-esteem to the next level.

Never Compare Apples with Oranges

It is true that "comparison is the thief's joy." no matter how hard you try or what you achieve, you will always find someone who is doing better than you. Can you compare a high-achieving swimmer with an undefeated tennis player? No! They both have different expertise and aims. The same is the case with you. Though the lives of people you see around or on social media often look quite fascinating and sometimes relatable, comparing yourself to them would be like comparing apples with oranges. You are unique, and you must embrace it. Imagine how boring life would have been if everything and everyone looked the same. The beauty of the world lies in its diversity; let's cherish it each day by accepting your uniqueness.

Reframe Your Flaws

What are flaws, really? They are just traits that are labeled because they do not meet already-set standards. If we start seeing our flaws differently, it will change our whole self-perception. For instance, shyness is often seen as a flaw, especially when you are in high school. But instead of feeling bad for being an introverted fellow, you can see it differently and tell yourself, "I am an observant and reflective being who takes time to understand people and situations and react accordingly." In this way, your focus would shift to the positive outcome of your personality trait.

Let Go the Illusion of Perfection

Accepting our flaws means that we are simply acknowledging our humanness. No one is perfect, whether you can see it or not, but everyone is struggling through their own set of weaknesses. To free yourself from the burden of unrealistic expectations, let go of the idea of perfectionism and admit that you do not have to ace everything to prove your worthiness. Keep your mind open to the possibility of making mistakes, learning from them, and moving on! It is not your perfection that makes you cool, but your ability to show compassion towards yourself and others around you.

How Can I Silence Self-Criticism and Cultivate Self-Acceptance?

You can run from external voices and criticism, but you can never outrun your inner self-critic. The only way to shut down that inner negative voice is through reframing your by patterns and cultivating self-acceptance.

Firstly, get rid of the all-or-nothing mentality. In every situation, we tend to pick sides—perfect or imperfect, success or failure, bad or good. Sometimes, when we are unable to meet our own expectations or those of others, we blame ourselves for falling short instead of giving ourselves the room to grow and learn. Life is not about winning or losing a rat race; it is about living the best version of yourself6 and this is what you should constantly remind yourself of.

Stop overgeneralizing: Reaching conclusions and generalizing outcomes as per our past negative events is natural, and we all tend to do this to protect ourselves from potential harm, but we can counter those thoughts by acknowledging the fact that nothing is permanent and static, so there is always a chance to create new outcomes.

Count the Positive: It is easy to fool our minds into believing what we want to believe in. For instance, in any critical situation, you can redirect your focus by counting the positive aspects involved. Say you have failed a test! It is disappointing to not see the desired results that you have worked for, but when you see this failure as an opportunity to relearn and attempt better next time, you make the best of that situation.

Practice positive affirmations: Our mindset is shaped by the things we feed it. It is just like a canvas, which takes the color of the paint applied to it. So, when you develop the habit of constantly feeding your mind with positive affirmations, it starts accepting those as y. our new reality while dismissing the negative thoughts. What type of positive affirmations should I use? I come across this question all the time. Affirmations are a way to put a stamp on a characteristic that you already have. Through positive affirmation, you highlight the strengths of your personality. For instance, if I tell myself, "I am capable and I am strong," that is a positive affirmation. You can create your own affirmations, like:

Your Ticket to A Positive Mindset

When we create a positive mindset, we shift our focus from dwelling on limitations to recognizing possibilities. This shift in perspective gives us the power to believe in our capabilities and approach challenges with a constructive attitude. Positive thinking is a catalyst for increased self-esteem that allows us to see setbacks as opportunities for growth.

Try Cognitive reappraisal

It is basically a fun way to change how we see a situation and focus on the positive outcomes. Do you want to try it? Watch a movie or TV show and find the good things in tough situations or think about what advice you would give the characters to make them feel better. Once you get the hang of it, use the same idea in your own life. Consider that tricky situations, might actually teach you important lessons or have some hidden benefits. It is a mindset makeover!.

The Three good things exercise

According to research conducted by Seligman, Steen, Park, & Peterson in 2005, a super easy way to boost your positive mindset is by thinking about and writing down three good things every day. It is a happiness hack that works both in the short and long term All you have to do is take a few minutes each evening to reflect on your life until you come up with three great things that happened. It is a simple but powerful way to bring more positivity into your life!

Imagine Your Best possible future

So, there is this study carried out by Sheldon and Lyubomirsky in 2006, and they found out that imagining and writing about your absolute best future can actually boost your positive mindset. All you need to do is set aside just 15 minutes of your day and start writing down what your dream future could look like. Forget about the negatives or what might go wrong; this is all about focusing on the amazing stuff that could go right. So, get a pen and paper, let your imagination run free, and create a picture of your best potential future. Who knows? It might just bring a smile to your face!

Overcome Your Doubts and Fears:

It is completely normal to grapple with uncertainty and anxiety about the future, social situations, or personal abilities. One great way to conquer these doubts is to create self-awareness. When you understand your strengths and weaknesses, you acknowledge that imperfections are a natural part of growth. So, set realistic goals for yourself and break them down into manageable steps. Accept challenges as opportunities for learning rather than potential pitfalls. Be with a supportive network of friends, family, or mentors who can offer guidance and encouragement. Do not be afraid to express your feelings and look for help when needed. Remember that everyone has fears, and courage is not the absence of fear but the ability to act in spite of it. Trust the process of self-discovery, be patient with yourself, and believe in your capacity to overcome obstacles. As you face doubt and fears head-on, you will find the resilient spirit within you that can turn uncertainties into stepping stones toward a brighter future.

Set and achieve personal goals:

It is not always our inability to achieve our goals that leads to failure; sometimes we develop unrealistic expectations of ourselves and eventually suffer from disappointment. If you truly want to progress and boost your confidence by achieving your goals, then be smart about it. And by smart, I just mean to be quick-witted, but it is a widely recommended technique to turn every ambition into reality.

SMART is an acronym for Specific, Measurable, Achievable, Relevant, and Time-bound goals. Whatever idea comes to your mind, dissect it according to those five factors. First, begin by specifying your goal. For instance, if you want to get fit, then specify your fitness goals as "running a 5000 in the next three months." This precisely indicates what you should work for.

Your goal has to be measurable as well. The 5000 target in the previous example is a definitive figure that you can measure as time goes by. Similarly, if you want to finish reading a book, you can quantify the progress and read 10 pages per day. This will help you track progress.

Achievability is another major factor to consider here. You cannot aim to win the Olympics without training and practice. So instead of eyeing the unachievable goals, turn your attention to aims you can pursue. Your time, resources, and abilities together tell you whether or not your goals are achievable.

The relevancy of your goal also matters here. If you really want to become a professional piano player, then setting goals to excel at every other instrument will only keep you distracted. Set goals that are relevant to your objectives and values. Do not follow others and what they do!

Putting a time cap in place is also necessary to achieve a goal. A deadline creates a driving force that keeps you motivated. This is how the human mind works! Without a set deadline and a sense of urgency, we forget to pay attention to what we started. If you want to get fit and in shape, then tell yourself to lose 10 pounds in the next two months.

You can use the following template to categorize and organize your goals according to the SMART formula and see how it works!

SMART

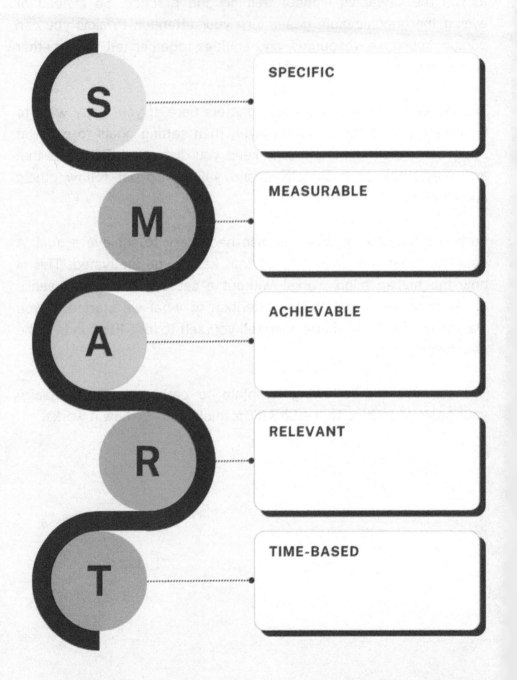

SPECIFIC

MEASURABLE

ACHIEVABLE

RELEVANT

TIME-BASED

Short-Term vs. Long-Term Goals?

Short-term goals are the stepping stones that help you achieve your long-term aspirations. They are the things you want to achieve in the near future, maybe in a matter of days, weeks, or a few months. For example, passing your upcoming math test, joining a school club, or finishing a book by the end of the month are short-term goals. On the other hand, long-term goals are the big dreams you are working for over an extended period of time like years. Graduating from high school, pursuing a specific career, or saving up for a car can be considered long-term goals. The key is to balance these goals and break down the long-term ones into manageable steps or short-term goals.

Create action plans:

Turning your dreams into reality is totally doable with a solid action plan. To begin, first be crystal clear about your goal, whether it is passing a big exam, excelling in a sport, or diving into creative work. Break it down into smaller, manageable steps, like chapters in a book. Set specific deadlines for each step, this keeps you on track. Think about what resources you need, such as books, equipment, and support from friends or family, and make a list. Be ready to adapt; life is unpredictable, so your plan might need tweaks along the way. Share your goal with someone you trust; they can cheer you on and keep you accountable. Finally, celebrate the small wins along the way; it is the fuel that keeps your motivation burning.

How to Boost Your Motivation?

It is highly important to stay motivated while working towards goals, and it requires consistent effort and the implementation of strategies to keep you focused and inspired. Here are some strategies that can help you:

- Be self-disciplined and create a schedule or routine. Make a consistent routine that includes dedicated time for working towards your goals. This will help you build a habit and make it easier to stay on track.

Visualize your success. Picture yourself achieving your goals. If you want to achieve a medal in the school volleyball championship, then visualize yourself receiving that medal in front of the whole crowd and feeling proud.

Stay Positive: Keep a positive mindset. Focus on what you have accomplished so far rather than what you have not. Positive self-talk can greatly impact your motivation.

Be with supportive people: Share your goals with friends, family, or mentors who can offer encouragement and support.

Reward Yourself: Treat yourself when you achieve milestones with a treat. Rewards can be small, such as taking a break, enjoying your favorite treat, or engaging in a relaxing activity.

Track your progress: Keep a record of all your achievements and progress. Reflect on how far you have come to remind you of your capabilities.

Mix It Up: Introduce variety into your routine and keep things interesting. Monotony can cause boredom and a decrease in motivation.

Stay Inspired: Continuously look for inspiration from sources such as books, podcasts, or role models. Learning from others who have achieved similar goals can fuel your motivation.

ACTIVITY 1: POSITIVITY JAR

Make a positivity jar. It is a wonderful way to develop self-love and boost your confidence. Here is a step-by-step guide to help you get started:

Materials You Will Need:
- A jar or container
- Small pieces of paper or sticky notes
- Pens or markers

Select any jar or container that you find appealing or meaningful. It could be a mason jar, a decorated container, or anything you have on hand. Cut small pieces of paper or use sticky notes. Make sure that they are small enough to fit comfortably inside the jar. Every day, take a few moments to reflect on your strengths, achievements, or positive qualities.

Write down three positive affirmations or compliments about yourself on separate pieces of paper. Fold each piece of paper and place it inside the jar. You can add a new note every day. Whenever you are feeling self-doubt or need a confidence boost, take a moment to read one or more affirmations aloud. This simple act reinforces positive self-talk and helps shift your mindset.

THE POWER

OF BEING

"YOU"

2

CHAPTER 2:

NAVIGATING RELATIONSHIPS AND FRIENDSHIPS

Have you ever found yourself wondering, "How do I deal with this situation?", "Am I a good friend?" or "What is up with all these emotions?" We get it; it is a crazy maze sometimes to deal with your emotions. But guess what? You are not alone in this whirlwind of emotions and feelings. Here is the deal: relationships can be tricky, and friendships can feel like they are unpredictable. But you got this! It might seem tough to steer through the ups and downs now, but by understanding your own emotions, you can develop the power of emotional intelligence to deal with friendship and relationship challenges. Be real with yourself, accept who you are, and stay confident. Trust me, it is nice to not have all the answers right away. You are learning, growing, and figuring out the complexities of relationships. Keep your head up! You are stronger than you think you are!

Talking So People Listen

So, you must have probably noticed it, right? Communication can get a bit tricky in our teenage years. The problem is that, as we grow, our needs to express ourselves also change. We need to upgrade our communication system to match our evolving selves. You need to learn fresh, effective methods for communication to not just impress your English teacher but to make sure that your squad catches your drift and you catch theirs. Whether it is dealing with crush drama, group projects, or just shooting the breeze, learning killer communication skills can unlock a new level in the game of high school life. So, let's upgrade those communication skills and conquer the teenage communication challenge together!

Clear Message: Keep it simple! Nobody likes decoding a secret message. Speak straight up, so everyone gets what you are saying.

Active Listening: When your friend talks, put down your phone and give them your full attention. Look them in the eye; show you are listening and not daydreaming.

Body Language: Your body talks too! If you are happy, let it show with a grin. If you are bored, try not to look like nap time is calling.

Respect: Be nice and polite. Use words that do not step on anyone's toes. Even if you are not vibing with someone, you can still keep it respectful.

Empathy: Feel what your friends are feeling. If someone's down, think about what could cheer them up.

Feedback: Check if you are on the same page. Repeat what you heard or throw in some questions. It stops the mix-ups.

Timing: Pick the right moment to drop the deets. If your bud just bombed a test, maybe do not flex about your awesome grades right then.

Open-mindedness: Stay open to different ideas. You do not have to agree on everything, but at least hear them out.

Confidence: Speak up, but do not go all shouty. Confidence is all about believing in what you are saying. Own your words, and do not be scared to share your thoughts.

Adaptability: Mix up your style based on who you are talking to. What flies with your crew might not jive with your teacher. Be flexible!

Humor: A good laugh is the best icebreaker. Just remember, not everyone laughs at the same jokes. Keep it chill and fun.

Active Listening for Enhanced Communication

When you listen actively, you are not just hearing the words; you are really tuning in. When you are vibing with active listening, you are not planning what to say next; you are totally in the moment, absorbing what your bud is throwing down. This extraordinary power helps you get the full scoop on what is going on. You pick up the feels, read between the lines, and show your crew that you are all ears. Active listening makes the conversation flow smoother than your favorite playlist. So, drop the distractions, look your friend in the eye, and let them know you are on the same wavelength. It is the key to leveling up your communication game in high school and beyond.

Techniques For Expressing Thoughts and Opinions Clearly

Expressing your thoughts seems harder than it looks. Even if you are a talker, you may find it difficult to put your opinions across, especially when you fear that others won't welcome them openly. Here is what you need to do!

Speak Up, Do Not Freak Out: Do not hold back your thoughts or opinions just because you are nervous. If you are in a group discussion, do not let fear stop you. For example, instead of staying quiet when your friends are deciding what movie to watch, suggest your favorite and explain why you like it.

Be Clear, Not Confusing: Avoid using complicated language or beating around the bush. State your thoughts in a straightforward manner. For instance, if you are discussing plans for the weekend, instead of saying, "Well, um, I was thinking, like, maybe we could, you know, go somewhere?" say, "I would love to go to the park this weekend. What do you think?"

Use "I" statements: express your feelings and thoughts from your perspective. For instance, instead of saying, "You never listen to me," say, "I feel like my opinions are sometimes overlooked, and it would mean a lot if I could share my thoughts too."

Stay Calm and Collected: Keep your emotions in check, especially during disagreements. For example, if someone disagrees with your viewpoint, rather than getting defensive, take a breath and calmly explain your perspective.

Find Common Ground: Look for shared interests or agreements. If you are discussing plans with friends and there is disagreement, then find a compromise. "We all like different music, but how about we take turns choosing songs?"

Consider Other Views: Put yourself in someone else's shoes. If you are discussing a controversial topic, understand that people may have different experiences that shape their opinions. For example, in a discussion about school policies, consider how the rules may affect students differently based on their experiences.

Ask Questions: Show interest in others' opinions by asking questions. If someone shares an idea you do not understand, ask for clarification. "Can you explain more about why you think that would be a good idea?"

Agree to Disagree: Accept that not everyone will share your views, and that is perfectly fine. If you can't agree on something, acknowledge the difference and move on. "I respect your opinion, even though I see it differently."

Assertiveness vs. Aggressiveness vs. Passiveness:

Assertiveness, aggressiveness, and passiveness are three key players in the communication game. Assertiveness is like the Goldilocks zone. It is speaking up for yourself, but without steamrolling others or fading into the background.

- **Aggressiveness,** on the other hand, is forceful, in-your-face, and can bulldoze over others. It is definitely not cool and does not add validity to your statements.

- **Passiveness:** Whereas, being passive is more like whispering when you should be speaking up. It is holding back, not sharing your thoughts, and letting others take the lead.

Why Being Assertive Rocks: It helps you build healthy relationships, whether it is with friends, family, or even your crush. When you are assertive, you are honest about what you want, you listen to others, and you respect their opinions too. It is the secret ingredient for creating great connections.

Balancing Act: Tips for Being Assertive:

Share your thoughts and feelings with confidence, but keep it chill. There is no need to go into full-on superhero mode.

Assertiveness is a two-way street. Listen up when others are talking and show that you value their opinions.

Instead of pointing fingers, talk about your own feelings and needs. It is less blamey and more about you.

Understand where others are coming from. It is the same as putting on their shoes and seeing the world through their eyes.

Know your limits and make them clear. It is not about building walls; it is about respecting yourself.

How to Handle Misunderstandings or Miscommunications?

Misunderstandings often step in when we assume, misinterpret, or do not express ourselves clearly. Texts, messages, and even in-person talks can sometimes lead to confusion. The key? Use the strategies for clarification. If you are unsure, ask questions, paraphrase, and make sure that you are on the same page as others.

Now, here is where empathy plays a huge role. Put yourself in the other person's shoes. Understand their perspective and feelings. This not only builds stronger connections, but it is also a powerful tool for resolving conflicts. Imagine it as a cooperative game where both sides work together to find common ground.

Surviving Peer Pressure and Dealing with Conflicts:

As the saying goes, "Be yourself; everyone else is already taken." Imagine yourself going through the exciting maze of teenage life and suddenly, peer pressure steps onto the scene, whispering its influence. It is a moment in a game where the plot takes an unexpected turn. The pressure is so real that it may give you anxiety and depression, so it is important to recognize and resist it. Imagine you are faced with a scenario where friends urge you to do something that does not align with your values. It is in these moments that standing firm becomes your power. Why? Because your journey, your choices, and your authenticity matter. Counteracting peer pressure is not just about saying "no" to others; it is about saying a resounding "yes" to yourself.

Different Types of Peer Pressure:

Now there are different forms of peer pressure that you must be aware of:

- **Direct Pressure**: The classic one - someone straight-up telling you to do something. Like a friend saying, "Come on, just try it!"

- **Indirect Pressure:** This is sneakier. It is when you feel influenced by seeing others do something and you think, "Maybe I should too."

- **Self-pressure**: Have you ever felt the need to fit in or be cool? That is self-pressure. You might do things just to be part of the crew, not because you actually want to do them.

Have you ever stopped to think about how peer pressure might be pulling the strings on your decision-making? There are many factors working at the back of this! Firstly, it is FOMO or the fear of missing out. It is this sneaky voice in the background telling you, "Do not miss out on the fun!" This fear can lead you to make choices you might not be comfortable with, just to stay in the loop and not miss a beat.

Next up, there is our innate desire for acceptance. We all want to be accepted, right? Well, peer pressure can crank up that desire, making us do things we might not usually do just to fit in and be part of the group.

Lastly, there is the lack of confidence factor. If you are not feeling super sure about yourself, your vulnerability meter goes off and you become susceptible to external voices. Peer pressure can act as a quick fix, making you lean towards what others are doing to feel more secure in the moment.

Positive Vs Negative Peer Pressure: Know the Difference!

The peer pressure is not always bad, it can be both negative and positive. Negative peer pressure is a dark cloud trying to push you into things that do not align with your values and they are potentially harmful. It is that voice saying, "Just do it, everyone else is." On the other hand, positive peer pressure is more of a supportive breeze nudging you toward healthy choices and growth. It is your friends encouraging you to study for that test or join a club that aligns with your interests. If your friends want you to go to a party but you are not comfortable then that's negative pressure working. Positive peer pressure would be to understand and say, "No worries, do what feels right for you." Or your study group is determined to ace the test, motivating you to work harder. That is positive peer pressure pushing you towards success. So, when you feel that pressure, take a moment to think, is it leading you down a path you are uncomfortable with or is it steering you toward positive growth? Trust your instincts and let your inner self guide you to make choices that assure you progress.

Conflict resolution strategies:

Conflicts are inevitable, believe it or not, and essential for our growth. They are unexpected challenges we face growing up. Rather than avoiding them, it is better to confront and handle them positively. Consider conflicts as opportunities to level up in your personal storyline. Confronting challenges head-on lets you learn, grow, and discover new things about yourself. So, do not press the escape button; accept this challenge with a positive mindset and resilience. Resolving conflicts does not have to be as challenging as defeating a final boss in a video game. In fact, there are some pretty easy ways to tackle conflicts:

Talk it out: The first step is to talk openly and honestly with the other person. Take it as a discussion of strategies to overcome a level in a game. If you and a friend disagree on plans, have a discussion about your preferences and find a compromise that works for both of you.

Listen Actively: Think of conflicts as a co-op game where everyone's input really matters. Actively listen to the other's perspective, just like you would pay attention to your teammate's strategy in a game. If there is a disagreement about chores, listen to each other's concerns to find a fair solution that benefits everyone.

Apologize and Forgive: In the game of conflicts, apologies are power-ups. If you make a mistake, apologize; there is no harm in it. And if someone apologizes to you, be ready to forgive and move forward. If you accidentally spill something on a friend's shirt, apologize sincerely, and if a friend apologizes for a misunderstanding, forgive and let it go. This will make your life much easier and stress-free.

Compromise: Conflicts often need a bit of compromise, like negotiating in a game. Find a middle ground that satisfies everyone involved. If you and a sibling want to watch different shows, compromise by taking turns or finding a show you both enjoy.

Take a Break: Conflicts can get intense at times. And if you continue to argue when your emotions are high, you might say things that are hurtful and unintentional. So, the best strategy is to take a break and hit the pause button. Step away, cool off, and return with a clear head to resolve the issue. If a disagreement with a friend gets too heated, take a break to calm down and revisit the conversation later.

Building Healthy Boundaries:

Here is a life skill worth mastering: creating healthy boundaries in friendships and relationships. Think of it like creating a fortress around your well-being. Having boundaries is crucial because it helps you define what is acceptable and comfortable for you. It is not about shutting people out but about valuing your own needs. Without your personal boundaries, people can step into your emotional and mental space and disrupt your peace and well-being.

The question is: how can you build those boundaries without stepping on anyone's toes? At first, communicate your need to have boundaries openly and honestly. Let your friends or partner know what you are comfortable with and what you are not. Learn to say "no" when needed. It is not a rejection; it is a way to prioritize your own well-being. You have the right over your personal time, space, and energy; people should only step into your personal space with your active permission. Just like in a game, you to make choices that lead to your victory. Listen to your instincts; they are your boundary radar. If something feels off, it probably is. So, trust yourself to make choices that align with your inner belief system.

Make Friends That Stick Around:

Your circle of friends is your support system. You know what they say: a man is known by the company he keeps. And that is one hundred percent true. With honest, supportive, caring, and sincere friends around, you can accomplish anything. The friends who stick around are your real keepers. Trust is the sturdy foundation of the friendship fortress, and it provides a sense of security. Loyalty is the glue that keeps your team together, no matter what challenges you face. Genuine support is the potion that fuels your collective strength. And fortunately, you can nurture and maintain these valuable friendships by staying authentic. Let your friends see the real you, complete with imperfections and quirks. Communication acts as your strategic guide, letting everyone be on the same page in this co-op play of life.

If you friends are being supportive then show appreciation for their contributions, much like celebrating achievements in a game. Acknowledge the little things they do that make a big difference. Lastly, be a stellar teammate yourself, offer them support, be reliable and contribute to creating memorable experiences together.

How To Deal with Changes in Friendships?

Suppose your best friend moves to a new city for a great education opportunity. This change might mean you will be physically apart, but your connection can still remain the same through calls and messages. Sometimes, new challenges or opportunities arise, which may lead to shifts in friendship dynamics. Perhaps your friend discovers a passion for a new hobby, and while your interests might differ, you both can still support each other's individual journey. Just as your character gains new skills, interests, or quests in the game, so do you and your friends. Accept these changes as part of the exciting journey of growing up.

Coping Strategies During Transitions or Difficulties:

Communication is your trusted map through these changes. Talk openly with your friends about how you are feeling and listen to their experiences too. Be open to making new friends as well. You will not be replacing old companions, but expanding your squad. Join clubs, engage in healthy activities, and meet people who share your current interests.

Plus, give yourself time to adapt. Change can be challenging, and it is okay to feel a mix of emotions. Just as characters need a moment to adjust to a new game environment, you too need time to settle into the shifts in your friendships. So, view changes as opportunities for growth, and remember, every friendship chapter contributes to the epic story of your life.

Being a Good Friend:

Being a good friend does not just mean sharing laughs and good times; it is also about offering support and understanding each other with kindness during both the highs and lows. True friendships are built on trust, honesty, and acceptance. To be a good friend, listen closely when your friends need someone to talk to, show empathy, and be non-judgmental. Celebrate their successes and be a source of comfort during challenging moments. Be reliable and dependable—someone they can count on. Respect their boundaries and differences that allow each of you to grow individually. Communication is key; express your feelings openly and encourage your friends to do the same. Be mindful of your actions and words, as they can have a lasting impact. Remember, being a good friend involves reciprocity; treat them the way you want to be treated. Ultimately, genuine friendships are a two-way street, and by being a supportive and caring friend, you contribute to creating a lasting and meaningful connection.

ACTIVITY 2: SHARE YOUR STORY

Sit together with your friends in a circle. Spin the bottle in the center; once it stops spinning, the person with the bottle head pointing towards him will have to share his or her story, a funny incident, or a challenging moment. This will help you connect with one another at a deeper level.

FRIENDSHIP
TRIALS

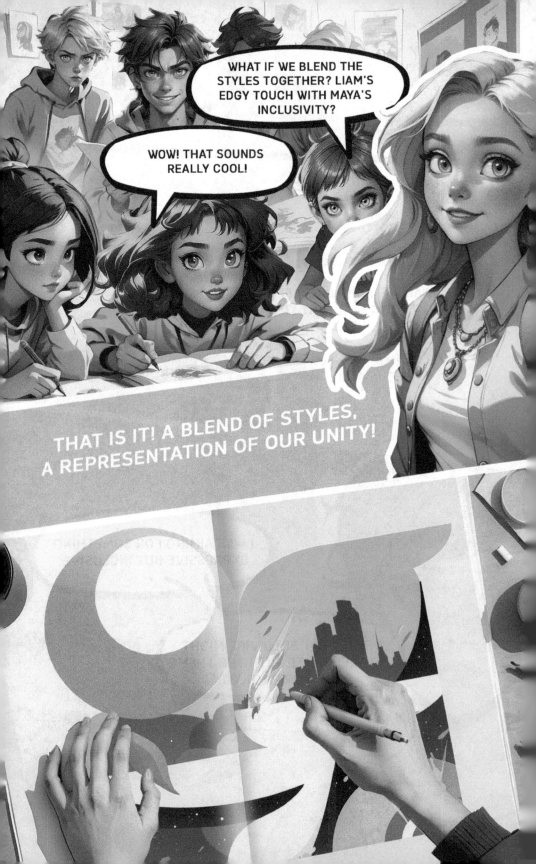

3

CHAPTER 3:

MONEY MOVES: CASH, COINS AND BUDGETS

Let's be honest here: money drama is no joke. We have all been there, feeling the struggle when that bank balance starts looking like a snack-run fund instead of a flex zone. But here is the deal: the key to dodging those money problems is to be straight-up smart about it. Budget like a boss! Make a plan for that paper; know where it is coming from and where it is going. Be real about your wants versus needs and resist the FOMO spending trap. Saving might sound lame, but trust me, the future will thank you and present you. And do not sleep on learning about investing. I just summed up. everything that we are about to learn in this chapter. It might sound too much or impossible to do everything that I have just explained here, but let me walk you through this process and show you how simple and easy it can get if you organize your income, spending, and funds. Let's roll out that cash!

Getting Smart About Cash:

Being smart about cash is totally within your control! It is not rocket science, just a combination of savvy moves and a sprinkle of smartness. Have you ever wondered what makes being smart about your money so crucial? Suppose you are eyeing that slick gaming console, and instead of going on an impulsive spending spree, you decide to save up for it. That is the magic of being smart with your money. It is not just about having cash in your pocket; it is about taking control of your financial state. By making intentional choices, setting spending goals, and understanding the impact of your spending, you are creating a secret financial power.

Needs vs Wants:

To control and change your spending habits, the very first step is to differentiate between your needs and wants. Unless you learn to be smart about your spending, you can never save enough money for the things that you really need. Needs are basically the essential things that are required for your survival, like food, shelter, and school supplies. Wants, on the other hand, are the nice extras that make life amazing, but they are not your must-haves. To slay your spending game, start by making a list of your monthly expenses. Ask yourself, "Is this a need or a want?" For example, getting a snack with friends is a want, while making sure you have lunch at school is a need. Be real about it: do you really need that new game console, or is it just a hype moment? Put your needs in order, budget for them first, and then keep some cash for your wants if there is room.

Be Financially Literate

Not understanding the basics of money would be like going into a battle without armor. You might get hit with overspending, debts around the corner, or unexpected expenses that feel like surprise enemy attacks. No one wants to be caught off guard, right? Fear not! With financial knowledge, you can take the ropes under your control. It is your ticket to creating budgets that actually work, saving up for your must-haves, and dodging the debt monsters. Suppose you have nailed a part-time gig, and instead of blowing all the cash on snacks, you store some for future shopping. Smart move, right? If you are ready to level up your money game, here is a lineup of amazing resources and books designed just for you.

Practical Money Skills for Life is your go-to website for interactive and comprehensive money education. It is packed with games, tools, and materials to teach you the ropes of budgeting, saving, and investing.

Khan Academy: Personal Finance: Have you ever wished personal finance could be as engaging as your favorite game? Khan Academy's personal finance courses make that a reality. Check out their free online courses which cover everything from budgeting to investing.

Cash Crunch Games: Turn your financial journey into a game with Cash Crunch Games. This app lets you step into real-life scenarios and makes learning about budgeting and decision-making a blast.

Bankaroo: Do you want to kick-start your virtual banking experience? Bankaroo is there for you. This app lets you track your allowances, set savings goals, and learn about money management in a super nice setting.

"The Total Money Makeover for Teens" by Dave Ramsey: It is your personal finance guide. It breaks down budgeting, saving, and avoiding debt into easy-to-follow steps.

"Smart Money, Smart Kids" by Dave Ramsey and Rachel Cruze: If you are looking for a dynamic duo to guide you through money lessons, this book is the right pick. This book is packed with valuable lessons on teaching you about money.

"I Will Teach You to Be Rich" by Ramit Sethi: It is your personal finance guru in book form. Geared towards young adults, this book covers everything from saving to investing.

"Get a Financial Life: Personal Finance in Your Twenties and Thirties" by Beth Kobliner:
It is your guide that can navigate you through the financial waters of your twenties and thirties. It covers budgeting, investing, and managing debt with real-life advice.

Responsible Spending and No Impulse Purchases

Let's say you are in the mall with your friends, and suddenly, you spot those flashy sneakers that seem to call your name. Without thinking twice, you decide, "Yep, I need those!" That, my friends, is impulse buying—the spontaneous purchases you do without really planning or thinking about it. Now, why does it matter? By controlling your impulse buying, you gain great control over your expenses. Instead of spending your hard-earned cash on things you did not really need or want in the first place, you get to be the boss of your spending decisions. Here are some simple hacks to control your impulses while spending your money!

The 24-Hour Rule:

Have you ever felt the urge to get something on impulse and later regretted it? Here is a trick—the 24-hour rule—and it is your secret weapon against impulse buying. The next time you are tempted to make a spontaneous purchase, hit the pause button and wait 24 hours before buying it. This gives you ample time to cool off, think it over, and decide if it is a need or just a passing want. For instance, imagine you spot a trendy pair of sneakers that seem like a must-have. Instead of buying right away, apply the 24-hour rule. If, after a day, you still think those kicks are a game-changer and worth the purchase, go for it. But often, you will find that the initial excitement fades away after a day, and you save your hard-earned cash for something truly worthwhile.

Make a shopping list:

Before hitting the stores or hopping online, write down exactly what you need. Be specific, whether it is snacks, school supplies, or that one thing you have been saving up for. Stick to the list like glue, and avoid wandering into the temptation zone of random purchases. For example, if you are headed to the mall for back-to-school shopping, write down the items you need, such as notebooks, pens, and a killer backpack. When you are armed with a list, you are in control, and you make intentional choices instead of falling for impulse purchases.

Smart Financial Habits in Our Daily Lives:

There are some healthy money habits that you need to develop in order to be financially sufficient. Start by setting aside a few minutes each day or week to check in on your spending. Use apps or pen and paper to track where your money is going. Next, make budgeting a part of your weekly or monthly routine. Break down your income and specify money for needs, wants, and savings. Now, here is the ninja move: whenever you get some cash, allocate a portion to your savings goals before anything else. For instance, if you earn $50 from a part-time gig, stash $10 into your savings before diving into other expenses. These small habits add up and keep you in control of your money.

Avoid debt traps:

Debt traps are the financial quicksand that pulls you in. You are at the mall, and a flashy credit card offer catches your eye. It promises the moon, but in reality, it is a sneaky trap with high interest rates and tricky terms. When you get tangled in debt at a young age, you create a tough cycle to break. What if you grab that credit card, start swiping for things you want but do not really need, and before you know it, you are stuck in a cycle of payments with interest adding up? However, when you avoid the debt traps, you empower yourself to make wise money choices, save for your dreams, and dodge the interest monsters.

Creating and Sticking to a Budget:

Budgeting is your secret weapon against those sneaky debt traps. Say you have your eye on the latest gaming console, and it is so tempting to whip out that credit card for an impulse buy. But hold up; that is where your budget steps in as your financial hero. By setting spending limits and planning your expenses in advance, you dodge the debt trap and save enough to buy the expensive things you like.

A Realistic and Effective Budget:

Your cash is like a VIP party, and you have to know who is coming in and who is going out. Here is how you can set a realistic budget by keeping an eye on your income and spending.

Calculate Your Income:

The first power move is to calculate your income. Start by tallying up all your income sources, allowances, part-time job earnings, or any other cash flowing your way. Let's break it down with an example: say you earn $100 a month from your part-time gig and get a $20 weekly allowance. Your monthly income is $100 + ($20 x 4 weeks) = $180. Armed with this knowledge, you can now plan your budget like a pro and decide how much goes to needs, wants, and savings.

List your expenses:

Now that you have calculated your income, the second step is to identify your expenses. List out all your regular expenses, such as lunch, transportation, and subscriptions. If your weekly lunch costs around $20 and you are shelling out $10 for transportation, that adds up to $30. With a monthly income of $180, deduct these regular expenses, and it will leave you with $150. Now, you have a clearer picture of where your savings are going.

Categorize your spending:

Organize your expenses into categories such as necessities, savings, and fun. For example, you might allocate $20 for necessities such as school lunch, transportation, and other essential stuff. Then, set aside $10 for savings. Finally, reserve $10 for fun activities; that could be a movie night, a snack run with friends, or whatever floats your boat.

Track your spending:

It is an amazing way to stay in control and avoid those unexpected plot twists in your finances. Start by writing down every single coin you drop, from that snack attack at the mall to the online splurge. Use apps, spreadsheets, or even a good old notebook—whatever floats your boat. Tracking helps you see where your money's really going and where you might need to tighten the purse strings. For example, if you notice you are dropping major coins on online shopping, you can adjust your plan and save that moolah for something bigger, such as a killer concert or a road trip with your friends.

Set savings goals:
Figure out what you are saving up for, whether it is a dreamy concert, a slick gadget, or a weekend getaway. Once you have your goal in mind, break it down into smaller, doable steps. Let's say your dream concert ticket is $100 and it is six months away. That is around $17 per month, which means that it is totally doable. Adjust your spending to make room for that goal. Keep your eyes on the prize. Having a goal keeps you focused on the bigger picture.

Save Smartly:
Make saving extra cash a habit, not just a one-time thing. Your savings are your backup squad, which stays ready to tackle any unexpected expense. Start small if you have to, such as stashing away a percentage of your allowance or part-time gig earnings. A nice move is to create a separate savings account if you can and watch that money grow like a boss. Let's say you aim to save $50 a month. Break it down to about $12.50 a week; that is like skipping a couple of fancy coffees. Trust me, when you hit your goal, the victory dance will be worth it.

Emergency Fund:
Life can throw curveballs at you, so having some emergency cash backup offers a shield for your wallet. Aim to save at least three to six months' worth of living expenses. In this way, you get a safety net for unexpected surprises like a broken phone or a surprise school trip. Treat your emergency fund like a sacred treasure; only use it when absolutely necessary. For example, if your monthly living expenses are around $200, try to build up a fund of $600 to $1200 over time. It might seem like a challenge, but when those

unexpected challenges pop up, you will be ready to slay without breaking a sweat.

Budgeting Strategies and Tools:

Budgeting might sound like a too-technical process that only grownups can do, but fear not; I have got your back! Think of it as a nice new skill that will set you up for a lifetime of financial prowess. I am about to spill the beans on some effective budgeting strategies that are your secret weapons for financial success.

Envelope System:

Have you ever heard of the envelope system? It is a budgeting technique that keeps your cash game strong and on point. First, identify your spending categories, which could be stuff like food, entertainment, or saving up for that sweet concert. Now, grab some envelopes and label each one with a category. Decide how much money you want to allocate to each category for the month. Once you have your cash, put the designated amount in each envelope. When it is time to spend, only use the cash in that specific envelope. Once it is empty, resist the urge to borrow from other envelopes, as that is the golden rule. For example, if you have set aside $50 for movies this month, only use the cash in the "Movies" envelope. It is a visual, hands-on way to stay on top of your spending and avoid budgeting chaos.

50/30/20 Rule:

If you are ready to level up your budgeting game, then use the 50/30/20 rule, which is a simple yet powerful strategy to keep your finances in check. Using this rule, you break down your income into three categories. First, allocate 50% of your cash for needs. Next, reserve 30% for wants, which is all the cool stuff that makes life awesome, such as gaming, dining out, or hitting up concerts. Lastly, stash away 20% for savings; your future self will thank you for this. Let me explain with an example. If your monthly income is $500, toss $250 into your needs bucket, keep $150 for wants (hello, Netflix and pizza nights), and stash away $100 into savings.

Budgeting Apps:

If you are not good at math and numbers, then you can also take the help of various mobile applications to process your numbers. Mint is the financial app that tracks your spending, sets budget goals, and even gives you a heads-up on bills. Simply connect your accounts, and Mint does the heavy lifting. If you are all about visualizing your budgeting journey, then try YNAB (You Need a Budget). It helps you allocate your cash to specific categories and makes sure every dollar has a job. Whereas if you want to save effortlessly, then Acorns is there to round up your everyday purchases to the nearest dollar and invest the spare change.

Adapting Budgets and Handling Challenges:

Changes are natural, and challenges are quests that help us grow. So, instead of running away from them, let's be smart and prepare in advance. Equip yourself with knowledge, skills, and a positive mindset. Some hiccups that you should look out for are:

Income Fluctuations:

Say your hours at the after-school job increase, giving you an extra $20 a week. You can add this surplus to your savings. Adapting to your income fluctuations is a skill that will serve you well on your financial journey. When the income tide is high, stash away a bit more to keep your emergency fund filled. If your income takes a temporary dip, focus on covering essentials such as food and school supplies before doing any discretionary spending.

Changing Priorities:

As your goals evolve, let your budget evolve too. Let's say you are all set to buy a concert ticket, but then the shiny allure of a new laptop catches your eye. No worries; adaptability is your power move. Shift gears, reallocate those funds, and watch your priorities take center stage. If you initially earmarked $30 for entertainment, but with the laptop dream in mind, you decide to dial it back to $10 for entertainment and redirect $20 to your savings.

Unexpected expenses or financial emergencies:

Facing unexpected expenses or financial emergencies can feel like a sudden plot twist in your financial journey. But fear not, because you have the skills to handle it like a champ. First things first, take a deep breath; panicking won't help. Assess the situation by identifying the urgency and the amount needed. If it is a smaller hiccup, like a sudden school project expense, consider adjusting your budget by reallocating funds from non-essential categories. For example, if your original budget allocated $30 for entertainment but the school project needs some financial attention, shift $15 from your entertainment budget to cover the unforeseen costs.

For more significant emergencies, like a broken phone or unexpected medical costs, having an emergency fund in place becomes your savior. If you do not have one yet, start setting aside a small portion of your income regularly to build it up. And remember, you are not alone; look for advice from your trusted adults or mentors.

If you are facing any financial challenges do not hesitate to talk to the people involved. Discuss your payment plans or alternatives if you can't meet a financial obligation. If you borrowed money from a friend but can't repay it on time due to unexpected expenses, communicate, explain the situation and work out a revised repayment plan. There is nothing that can't be solved with an honest discussion.

Common Pitfalls in Budgeting and How to Overcome Them:

Budgeting is not always a smooth ride. You might encounter a few bumps along the way, and guess what? That is absolutely okay! Here is how you can overcome those pitfalls!

Underestimating Expenses:

It is easy to get caught up in the hype of budgeting for fun stuff, but those everyday expenses can pose a challenge. Let's assume you budgeted $30 for snacks, thinking you are a snack master, but suddenly find yourself with a $50 craving because your favorite munchies are on sale. Boom, there goes the budget. The trick is to be real with yourself. When planning, overestimate your expenses a bit and round up instead of down. Give yourself a buffer zone for the unexpected. If snacks usually cost you $40, budget for that instead of $30. That way, when the sale hits, you are still in the clear.

Impulse Buying:
Let's tackle the budgeting villain we all know too well: impulse buying. It is a sneaky ninja that can wreck your financial plan if you are not careful. One day you are scrolling online and you spot those fresh kicks, and BAM, they are in your cart before you even blink. The key to overcoming this ninja move is to pause and reflect. When the impulse hits, take a breath. Ask yourself, "Do I really need this right now?" Consider if it aligns with your budget goals. Another trick is to implement a waiting period, as we discussed in the 24-hour rule. If you still want it after a day or two, go for it.

Ignoring the Emergency Fund:
It is tempting to think we are invincible, but life's unexpected quests can hit you hard. You are cruising through the month, then suddenly your phone decides to take a dive into the toilet. Without an emergency fund, you might find yourself scrambling to cover the costs. The remedy is to treat your emergency fund as your sidekick. Always allocate a small percentage of your income towards it each month. Even if it is just $20 or $30, it adds up over time. When the unexpected hits, like a phone emergency, you will have a financial shield to protect you.

Dodging money troubles:
Money troubles are the occasional rain in life; they happen to everyone. But you do have the power to dodge most of them by being smart about your money. It is the umbrella for your financial toolkit.

Recognize financial risks:

Start by staying informed and keeping an eye on the economic landscape, global events, and financial news. Be vigilant against scams in the online world, always verifying sources before sharing any personal or financial information. Watch out for debt. While it can be a tool, accumulating too much can pose risks to your financial well-being. Educate yourself continuously about personal finance; the more you know, the better equipped you are to identify potential risks.

Beware of Credit Card Traps:

Credit cards might look tempting and offer a gateway to instant purchases, but watch out for the hidden dangers. If you do not pay off the full amount each month, those interest charges start piling up. Before you know it, you are stuck in a money quicksand, juggling payments and trying to escape the cycle of debt.

Student Loan:

College is an exciting time, but student loans can stick around for a while. Pick a repayment plan that fits your future paycheck, so you are not drowning in debt after graduation.

Credit Score:

Your credit score is your financial report card; it determines your credibility. Missed payments can give you a bad grade, making it tough to get a loan or rent an apartment later. A credit score is a numerical representation of your creditworthiness. It varies from 300 to 850. The higher the score, the better. Your credit score matters because it can impact your ability to get a loan, rent an apartment, or even land a job. Lenders use it to assess the risk of lending to you. A higher score often means you are seen as a lower-risk borrower.

For you, building credit usually starts when you get your first credit card or take out a loan. Responsible use, like making timely payments, contributes positively to your credit history.

Credit Score Range:
300–579: Poor
580–669: Fair
670–739: Good
740–799: Very Good
800–850: Excellent

You are entitled to a free credit report annually from each of the major credit bureaus (Equifax, Experian, and TransUnion). Review it to ensure accuracy and catch any potential issues early. Avoid maxing out credit cards, pay bills on time, and be cautious when opening new lines of credit. These habits contribute to a healthy credit score.

Social Media Real Talk:
Social media is a dazzling showcase of fancy stuff, but not everyone's sharing their financial struggles. Do not let the online glam trick you into spending beyond your means. Focus on your journey, be smart about your money, and avoid falling into the trap of keeping up with unrealistic online standards.

Building Financial Resilience:

If you see your money not just as a means to buy stuff but as a tool to achieve your dreams, you are on the right track. With long-term financial resilience, you can create a sturdy shield for your money. Start by developing healthy money habits early on. Invest your time in learning about smart financial decisions, like understanding the basics of investing and building a diversified portfolio.

Avoid the lure of quick fixes and scams; instead, focus on building a sustainable and secure financial future. Education is your ally, so keep learning about personal finance, economic trends, and smart money moves. Diversify your income streams through side gigs or turning your hobbies into money-making ventures to add layers to your financial resilience. Finally, stay adaptable. Life's journey is dynamic, and being flexible in your financial strategies ensures you can navigate through the twists and turns with confidence.

Long-Term Financial Planning:

Financial planning is like playing a board game. Early, smart moves set the stage for victory. Similarly, early financial planning sets the groundwork for a stable and stress-free future. By saving and investing at a young age, you give your money more time to grow. Financial freedom gives the room to make various choices. Whether it is pursuing your dream job, starting a business, or traveling the world, a solid financial foundation gives you the power to make decisions based on passion, not just necessity.

The first step is to explore the world of investments. Investments such as stocks or mutual funds have the potential to grow your money over the long term. But remember, investments need attention and monitoring. As teens, you cannot invest a huge amount or take huge risks, but if you have some extra money, then look for low-investment options to kickstart your financial journey:

Savings Account: Open a savings account to park your savings. While interest rates may be modest, it is a safe way to start building a financial foundation.

Certificate of Deposit (CD): CDs offer slightly higher interest rates than regular savings accounts, lock your money for a specific period, and offer a small return on your investment.

High-Yield Savings Account: Some online banks offer higher return rates on savings accounts compared to traditional banks. Explore these options for better returns on your savings.

Stock market via ETFs: Exchange-traded funds (ETFs) let you invest in a diverse range of stocks with a single purchase. It is a way to dip your toes into the stock market with a relatively small investment.

Start a Side Hustle: Invest your time and skills in a side hustle, whether it is freelancing, tutoring, or creating and selling crafts. The initial investment may be minimal, and it is an opportunity to earn and learn.

Online Courses: Invest in yourself by taking online courses. Many platforms, like Coursera, Udemy, Google, LinkedIn, etc., offer affordable or even free courses that can enhance your skills and knowledge, potentially leading to future financial opportunities.

Dividend Stocks: Some companies pay dividends to their shareholders. Invest in stocks that offer dividends, and over time, you can reinvest those dividends to grow your investment further.

If someone has advised you to invest in cryptocurrency, then I would recommend you think twice before taking the leap. While cryptocurrency investments seem quite lucrative, they require in-depth knowledge, experience, and lots of time to make a profit. Without a sound understanding, jumping into it can be a bit risky, so be cautious!

ACTIVITY 3:
LET'S CREATE A BUDGET PLANNER

Create a weekly budget planner, use the template given below, and add entries each day to keep track of your expenses, saving goals, and emergency funds.

Budget Planner

NAME:	DATE:

My Income

DATE:	DESCRIPTION:	AMOUNT:

My Expense

DATE:	DESCRIPTION:	AMOUNT:

Notes

TOTAL EXPENSE

TOTAL INCOME

TOTAL SAVINGS

BUDGET BUMPS

4

CHAPTER 4:

SECRETS TO SCHOOL SUCCESS AND WINNING AT LEARNING

How is everything going on the academic front? Are you feeling confident and satisfied with your progress in school? Learning is a journey, and sometimes we all need a little extra boost to get through it successfully. The workload, exams, and constant tests can create a whirlwind of stress. Balancing diverse subjects and assignments may lead to time management struggles, and that makes it difficult to juggle all your priorities effectively. The pressure to perform well can be overwhelming, especially when expectations are high. Plus, finding motivation during periods of fatigue or distraction can pose a challenge. Let me tell you that you are not alone in facing these academic hurdles; many of you share similar experiences. And fortunately, there are also some smart and intelligent ways to nail your academic progress without beating yourself over it.

Study and Time Management Skills:

Academic progress and time management go hand in hand. Getting your homework done, preparing for exams, and tackling projects all come down to how you manage your time. Trust me, finding that sweet spot between study sessions, fun time, and maybe a movie binge is key.

Effective Study Habits:

Do you feel the pre-test jitters? I totally get it! It feels like your brain is going on a trampoline. Remember that you have the power to ace that test with some game-changing study habits. First off, break down your study sessions into bite-sized pieces. Then follow the following habits:

Remember with spaced-out practice: Do not cram all your studying into one session. Spread it out over time. Review what you have learned at increasing intervals. This helps you remember things for the long term.

Make Visual Maps: Draw pictures or diagrams to see how different ideas are connected. Start with a main idea in the middle and add branches for related topics. It helps you see how everything fits together.

Take Small Bites: Break big amounts of information into smaller parts. Focus on one piece at a time before moving on. It makes things less overwhelming and helps you understand and remember better.

Practice by Testing Yourself: Test your knowledge regularly. Use flashcards, take practice quizzes ,or solve problems related to what you are learning. This helps reinforce what you remember and shows you what you need to review.

Mix Things Up: Use different ways to learn. Read, listen, watch videos, or talk about ideas with friends. Using different methods helps you understand and remember better.

DAILY STUDY SCHEDULE

(DAY/DATE:)

(07:00) _____
(08:00) _____
(09:00) _____
(10:00) _____
(11:00) _____
(12:00) _____
(13:00) _____
(14:00) _____
(15:00) _____
(16:00) _____
(17:00) _____
(18:00) _____
(19:00) _____
(20:00) _____
(21:00) _____
(22:00) _____

(MAIN GOAL)
_____
_____
_____
_____
_____

(TESTS)
_____
_____
_____
_____
_____

(SUBJECTS TO FOCUS)
(____)
(____)
(____)
(____)

(PREPARED FOR)   (YES) (NO)

_____   ( )   ( )
                        ( )   ( )
_____   ( )   ( )
                        ( )   ( )
_____   ( )   ( )
                        ( )   ( )
_____   ( )   ( )
                        ( )   ( )

(NOTE TO SELF)
_____
_____
_____
_____

Make flashcards: Flashcards let you recall the learned ideas effectively. They have the questions on one side and the answers on the other. You can sit with your friends to revise the concepts by using the flashcards. When you make the flashcards, you get to revise the concepts.

Stick to a schedule: Have a regular study routine. Doing this helps your brain know when it is time to focus. Consistency is extremely important for doing well over a long period of time. For instance, your can schedule you timetable like this.

Sort Out Your Time: Figure out what is most important and needs to be done first. Managing your time well means you give each subject or task enough time, which reduces stress and helps you work more efficiently.

How to improve your focus?

- Create a specific area for studying that is quiet, comfortable, and free from distractions. Make sure it is well-lit and organized, creating a conducive environment for concentration.
- Silence your phone or turn off non-essential notifications on your devices. This minimizes the chances of being interrupted by calls, messages, or social media alerts.
- Identify the most important tasks and tackle them first. Prioritizing helps you focus on what truly matters and prevents feeling overwhelmed by a long to-do list.
- Divide larger tasks into smaller, more manageable segments. This makes the workload seem less daunting, and you can focus on completing one step at a time.
- Develop a study schedule and stick to it. Having a routine helps train your brain to be ready for focused work during specific times.
- Consider using productivity tools and apps that can help you stay on track. Tools such as website blockers or apps that limit your access to distracting content can be beneficial.

Schedule short breaks between study sessions to prevent burnout. Use this time to stretch, walk around, or do something enjoyable to recharge your energy.

Some people find that low-volume background music or white noise helps drown out potential distractions and improves concentration. Experiment to see what works best for you.

Let those around you know when you need focused study time. Communicate your boundaries to reduce interruptions and create a supportive environment.

Time Management Strategies:

Managing your time is super important when it comes to doing well in exams and tests. Think of it like getting better at a video game; you need skills to tackle challenges, and time management is a big one. When you are good at it, studying becomes a fun thing. Whether it is a big exam or a surprise quiz, how you handle your time is the real test.

Pomodoro Technique:

Francesco Cirillo created this useful time management technique in the late 1980s. Using this techniques you break your work into intervals, for instance 25 minutes in length, separated by short breaks. These intervals are called "Pomodoros." After completing four intervals of Pomodoros, take a longer break of 15–30 minutes. This strategy is useful in improving focus and productivity by utilizing the benefits of short bursts of intensive work followed by brief periods of respite.

To-Do Lists:

To-do lists are a classic time management tool. Create a list of tasks you need to accomplish and organize them by priority or deadline. Start with the most critical tasks to ensure they are completed first. As you complete each item, cross it off the list. To make your to-do list even more effective, break down larger tasks into smaller and more manageable sub-tasks.

To do list

Priorities:

1. _____ 2. _____ 3. _____

✔	✗		Notes

✔ ✗

○ ○ _____

○ ○ _____

○ ○ _____

○ ○ _____

○ ○ _____

○ ○ _____

○ ○ _____

○ ○ _____

○ ○ _____

○ ○ _____

○ ○ _____

○ ○ _____

○ ○ _____

○ ○ _____

○ ○ _____

Notes

For tomorrow

Time Blocking:

In time blocking, you schedule specific blocks of time for different tasks or activities throughout the day. Allocate a dedicated time period for work, meetings, breaks, and personal activities. By allocating fixed periods to specific tasks, you create a structured routine that helps minimize multitasking and increases focus. Use a calendar or planner to visualize your time blocks. This technique promotes your productivity by providing a clear roadmap for the day.

Eat That Frog:

Brian Tracy presents the idea of "Eat That Frog" in his book. The idea is to deal with your most challenging or important task first thing in the morning, and it is metaphorically referred to as "eating the frog." By addressing the most demanding task early in the day, you set a positive tone. This technique helps prevent procrastination and promotes a sense of accomplishment.

Limit Distractions:

Identify and minimize distractions to maintain focus and productivity. Turn off mobile notifications while studying, create a separate workspace, and communicate your needs with your family for uninterrupted time. You can also use productivity tools or apps that block distracting websites or social media during work periods.

Say No:

Learn to say no to additional commitments or tasks that do not align with your priorities or goals. Put your existing responsibilities on top of the list and understand that saying no is an imperative for maintaining a healthy school-life balance. Politely decline requests that would overextend your time, energy and allow you to focus on what truly matters.

Use Apps:

Use the digital productivity app to organize your tasks, deadlines, and appointments. Choose a system that suits your preferences, such as Trello, Todoist, or Google Calendar. Add all your tasks, events, and deadlines to the planner, and regularly review and update it. With a centralized place for information, you can easily organize your tasks.

Reward Yourself:
Reward yourself for completing tasks or reaching milestones, as it provides positive reinforcement and motivation. Identify specific rewards that align with your preferences and values. After accomplishing a significant task, take a break, treat yourself to a small indulgence, or engage in a leisure activity. This technique helps create a positive association with completing tasks and can contribute to sustained motivation over the long term.

Goal-Oriented Approach to Learning:
Define short-term and long-term objectives, making them measurable and achievable. Break larger goals into smaller milestones to track progress. Regularly review and adjust your goals to stay aligned with your priorities. Goal-setting provides a sense of purpose, guiding your actions and decisions. Remember the SMART criteria we discussed in Chapter 1? Use them to make sure that your goals are well-defined and realistic.

One way to stay motivated is to set periodic milestones within your larger academic goals. Celebrate small victories, whether it is mastering a challenging concept, completing a chapter, or achieving a high score on a practice test. Recognize your efforts and progress regularly. Plan enjoyable breaks, treat yourself to a favorite snack, or engage in a leisure activity after reaching a significant milestone. These rewards create a positive association with academic work, making it more likely that you will stay motivated and committed to your goals over time.

Ace Tests Without Stress:
It is a chilly evening, and you find yourself sitting at your desk in your room, with textbooks, notebooks, and a laptop scattered around. Tomorrow is a big day, and anxiety is creeping in. There is an important biology test covering various chapters, and you are

unsure how to approach it. Now there are two ways to deal with this situation! To panic, procrastinate, and find refuge in Instagram reels, you can use the time available, be organized, and use the following techniques to prepare well: The second method is going to help you ace your stress, and the first will leave you feeling stressed. Which one would you choose? Of course, the second one!

Effective Test Preparation

Begin your preparation well in advance to avoid last-minute cramming. Gather all necessary textbooks, notes, and resources. Have everything in one place to streamline your study process. Develop a realistic study schedule that covers all relevant topics. Allocate more time to challenging subjects or those with greater weight in the exam. Simulate exam conditions during practice tests. Practice managing your time effectively to ensure you can answer all questions within the allotted timeframe. Regularly review and revise previously studied material to reinforce your understanding. Focus on weak areas to strengthen your overall knowledge.

Create A Tailored Study Plan for Upcoming Tests

Understand your exam format, the topics covered, and any specific areas emphasized by the instructor. Divide the material into smaller, manageable sections. This helps prevent feeling overwhelmed and allows for focused study. Determine the importance of each topic. Focus on high-priority areas, but do not neglect less-emphasized content. Make achievable goals for each study session. This could include completing a certain number of practice problems or thoroughly understanding a specific concept.

Suppose you are preparing for a history exam, and the first step is to understand the exam format, topics covered, and specific areas your instructor emphasized. After reviewing the syllabus and any guidance provided, you identify key themes such as historical events, influential figures, and critical concepts.

Next, you divide the extensive material into smaller sections. Instead of tackling the entire history of a specific era at once, you break it down into distinct periods, focusing on one at a time. This approach prevents you from feeling overwhelmed and allows for more concentrated and effective study sessions.

Now, you need to determine the importance of each topic. While studying the Renaissance might be crucial, your instructor may have highlighted certain aspects, like the impact of art on society. Recognizing these high-priority areas helps you direct your efforts appropriately, but it is essential not to neglect less-emphasized content entirely. This ensures you have a well-rounded understanding of the subject matter.

Strategies for Managing Test Anxiety and Staying Calm During Exams:

Let's talk about something we have all felt at some point: test and exam anxiety. It is real, and it is totally okay to feel a bit jittery before hitting the books. The key is acknowledging that those nerves are natural, but it is equally important to calm them down before diving into your study sessions.

- **Deep Breathing:** Take a moment to do some deep breaths. Breathe in slowly, hold for a bit, and then let it out. Hit the reset button for your mind and kick stress to the curb.

- **Positive Self-Talk:** When those negative thoughts creep in, shut them down with some positive vibes. Remind yourself that you have prepped for this and you aced things before.

- **Visualization:** Let's think of yourself totally rocking that exam. Picture each question as a victory waiting to happen. This mind trick builds up your confidence and knocks anxiety out of the park.

- **Arrive Early:** Beat the stress game by getting to the exam early. It gives you time to chill, find your Zen, and read through the instructions without any last-minute panic.

- **Focus on the present:** Do not let the whole exam stress you out. Take it one question at a time. Stay in the zone, concentrate on the task in front of you, and soon you will be acing it without even realizing it.

- **Prepare physically:** pack your gear, pens, pencils, and ID, and be ready to conquer. Being physically ready means less stress when the exam moment arrives.

Test-Taking Strategies:

When it comes to tests and exams, time is your secret weapon! Manage it wisely to make a huge difference in your performance. Suppose the clock is ticking, questions are waiting, and you are in control. So, here is the deal: set mini-goals for each part of the test, keep an eye on the clock (yes, bring a watch or use your phone), and start with the questions you find easier to build some early confidence. Do not get stuck on one question; if it is tricky, skip it and come back later.

Chunking: Break down large amounts of information into smaller, manageable chunks or groups. If you are trying to remember a long string of numbers like 482916547, you might chunk it into smaller groups like 482, 916, and 547, making it easier to remember.

Association: In association, you connect new information with something you already know or are familiar with, creating mental links between the old and the new. If you are learning a new language and come across the word "maison," you might associate it with the English word "house" to make a connection.

Mnemonics: In mnemonics, you associate, often in the form of acronyms, rhymes, or vivid phrases, to aid in remembering lists or sequences. To remember the order of the planets in our solar system

(Mercury, Venus, Earth, Mars, Jupiter, Saturn, Uranus, and Neptune), you might use the mnemonic "My Very Educated Mother Just Served Us Noodles," where the initial letter of each word corresponds to a planet.

Visualization: Create mental images of concepts or information to enhance memory recall. If you are studying the parts of a cell, visualize each part in its location; picture the nucleus as the "control center" and the mitochondria as the "powerhouse."

Active Recall: Actively test yourself on the material without looking at notes or textbooks. This process reinforces memory by forcing your brain to retrieve information. Instead of simply re-reading your notes, cover them up and try to recall the key concepts. This might involve answering questions about the material or explaining it as if you were teaching it to someone else.

Time Management and Pacing During Tests

- Quickly scan through the entire test before starting. Note the types of questions, point values, and any instructions. This provides a roadmap for allocating your time.

- Begin with the questions you find easiest and are most confident about. This helps you gain momentum and build confidence early in the test.

- Assign specific time limits for each section or question based on its point value. This prevents spending too much time on one question at the expense of others. For example, if you have an hour for a four-section test, allocate 15 minutes to each part.

- Bring a watch or use a timer if allowed. Keep track of time to ensure you stay within your planned limits for each section.

- If you get stuck on a question, do not spend too much time pondering. Skip it and return later if time allows. Focusing on what you know first boosts overall productivity.

- If time permits, go back and review your answers. Check for errors, provide additional detail if needed, and ensure you have answered all parts of each question.

- Periodically glance at the clock to gauge your progress. This prevents you from running out of time unexpectedly and allows you to adjust your pace if necessary.

- Allocate time based on the point value of each question. Do not spend an excessive amount of time on a low-point question that could be better used on higher-point questions.

- If you feel time pressure, take a deep breath. Stay calm and focused. Panic can hinder your ability to think clearly, so maintaining composure is crucial.

- Practice relaxation techniques before and during the test. Deep breathing or positive affirmations can help manage test anxiety, ensuring better concentration on the task at hand.

- For essay questions, outline your response before diving in. This brief planning stage helps organize your thoughts, ensuring a more efficient and coherent answer.

- Carefully read and understand all instructions before starting. Misinterpreting instructions can lead to mistakes that cost valuable time.

Recovery From Test Setbacks:

We have all been there; a test does not go as planned, and it feels like a major setback. First off, it is okay to feel disappointed. Give yourself a moment to absorb it, but do not let it define you. Instead of dwelling on what went wrong, focus on what you can do differently next time. Remember, one test does not determine your worth or potential. Use it as a chance to learn and grow.

Okay, let's turn those setbacks into comebacks! Start by reviewing your test, seeing where you stumbled, and understanding why. Were there specific topics that tripped you up? Did time management play a role? Use this information to tweak your study approach. Create a plan; maybe it is more practice questions, a study group, or seeking help from your teacher.

If the struggle feels real, do not hesitate to look for help or support. Talk to your teachers; they are there to guide you. A study buddy can bring fresh perspectives, and your friends might have genius tips. Do not be shy about asking questions or admitting when you are stuck. Everyone faces challenges, and reaching out for help is a strength, not a weakness.

Balancing Academics with Extracurricular Activities:

Life is one big juggling act, and finding the balance between academics and extracurricular activities is key. It is not just about acing tests; it is about exploring your passions, making memories, and growing into a well-rounded individual. Join a club, play a sport, or dive into an art project; these experiences not only add color to your life but also teach you skills that go beyond textbooks.

Prioritize Your Commitments

Start by understanding your academic workload, upcoming tests, assignments, and projects. What needs your immediate attention? Then, look at your extracurriculars—are they something you are passionate about or just filling up your schedule? Consider what contributes to your growth and happiness. When you are in study mode, give it your all. When it is time for your club or sports practice, immerse yourself in the experience. Learn to switch gears without feeling guilty; it is all part of the harmony. Sometimes it means tough decisions, but finding that equilibrium ensures you are not just succeeding academically but enjoying the journey too.

Impact on Academic Performance:

Extracurricular activities are the sprinkles on your academic cupcake; they can add some serious flavor! Joining clubs, sports, or the arts can positively influence your academic performance by boosting your time management skills. When you are diving into extracurricular activities, set clear boundaries. Create a realistic schedule that accommodates both study time and your passions. Regularly assess your commitments to ensure they align with your academic goals. Remember, it is about harmony, not piling on more than you can handle.

Your extracurricular adventures are not just fun; they are skill-building boot camps! Whether you are leading a club or playing a sport, the leadership, teamwork, and problem-solving skills you gain can supercharge your academic success. Use these experiences to enhance your resume, make connections with what you are learning in class, and even find unique angles for assignments.

Maintaining Balance and Boundaries:

Life's a mixtape! To maintain a healthy balance between school and your extracurricular passions, try scheduling dedicated study blocks and activity times. Think of your time and energy as a precious resource; you would not spend them all in one place. Create boundaries by setting realistic goals for both academics and extracurriculars. Be mindful of your limits and know when to say 'enough.' Schedule downtime, because recharging is as crucial as your hustle. Recognize the signs of burnout, exhaustion, and lack of motivation, and adjust your commitments accordingly.

We all need backup sometimes, and that is totally cool. When the academic and extracurricular rollercoaster feels overwhelming, lean on your support squad. Talk to teachers or mentors about your challenges. Share your feelings with friends and family; they have got your back. Explore resources like time management apps or counseling services at school.

ACTIVITY 4: TEACH A FRIEND

Divide the subjects among you and your friends, and assign each individual a topic to teach the rest. Make flashcards, PowerPoint presentations, or visual aids to explain the topic to your friends.

EXAM STRESS

5

CHAPTER 5:

DIGITAL CITIZENSHIP AND ONLINE SAFETY

"With great power comes great responsibility." In our digital age, the internet is a powerful tool, but it is imperative to handle it with care. Imagine you post something online, thinking it is just for friends, but it ends up in the wrong hands, causing unexpected consequences. That is the reality we face if we are not mindful of our online presence. The online universe is vast, and it offers endless opportunities for learning, connecting, and having fun. However, there are potential dangers lurking. From cyberbullying and online scams to inappropriate content and privacy concerns, the internet has its fair share of pitfalls. It is essential to be aware that not everything online is as it seems, and not everyone you encounter has good intentions.

Using social media Responsibly

Social media is a double-edged sword; it is great but comes with challenges. The benefits are endless: connecting with friends, exploring interests and even learning new things. However, risks like cyberbullying and privacy concerns are there. To use social media responsibly and maintain a positive digital footprint. Post things that showcase your interests, and achievements while steering clear of negative content. Follow the golden rule: treat others as you want to be treated. Be mindful of your privacy settings, use strong passwords, and think twice before sharing personal details. Keep it positive, keep it smart; your online world is what you make of it.

Healthy Online Interaction:

Being great on social media starts with how well you communicate. Keep it respectful and positive. If you disagree with someone, express your thoughts calmly without resorting to personal attacks.

Remember, online words carry weight, so choose them wisely. Use emojis or GIFs to add some good vibes, and if things get heated, consider taking a break before responding. Your online space is your vibe; make it a positive one!

The best way to deal with conflicts or disagreements:

Conflicts happen even in the digital world. When disagreements arise, take a deep breath. Responding in anger can escalate things. So, move the conversation to a private message to avoid a public showdown. If it gets too much, know when to step back. Report harassment or block it if necessary. Conflicts are part of life, but how you handle them online defines your digital character.

Avoiding Pitfalls of Comparison or Negative Influences:

Social media is a highlight reel, not the whole story. It is easy to fall into the comparison trap, feeling like everyone's life is perfect except yours. Remember, people share their best moments, not their struggles. If someone's content makes you feel negative, unfollow or mute them. Curate your feed to inspire and uplift you. Real life is way more than filters and likes, so do not let the digital world dictate your happiness!

Managing Privacy Settings

Manage your privacy settings on social media to put up a fence around your digital castle. It is super important! These settings determine who sees your posts and personal information and who can send you friend requests. Take the time to explore the settings on each platform and customize them based on your comfort level. Be selective; not everyone needs to know everything about you.

How can you control the content you share?

You should value your privacy and not share everything about your personal life online. Be mindful of geotagging, as it reveals your location and might put you in danger. Think before posting your photos or comments, and consider the potential impact on your reputation. Regularly audit your posts and remove anything that does not align with your current mindset.

Tips for Avoiding Oversharing Personal Information on Social Media?

- Check Your Privacy Squad: Be the boss of your online space! Set your privacy settings to control who sees your posts. Keep it tight and only let your real friends in.

- Friend Requests: Only buddy up with people you actually know. Avoid the mystery requests; you will be keeping your VIP party exclusive.

- Think Before You Snap and Share: Hold up before hitting that post button. Ask yourself, "Would I want my grandma to see this?" If not, maybe keep it to yourself.

- Keep Your Whereabouts on the Down: Turn off location sharing for social media apps. There is no need to let the world know where you are every second.

- Top Secret Stuff Stays Top Secret: Do not spill the tea on sensitive stuff; your address, phone number, and all that jazz should stay off the public stage.

- Untag: Keep an eye on tagged photos and posts. If something feels off, untag yourself, like a digital escape move.

- Slide into DMs for Personal Chats: Keep your inside jokes and personal chats in the DMs. Public posts are for high-fives, not heart-to-hearts.

- Watch Out for App Sneakiness: Those third-party apps can be sneaky. Be careful who gets access to your social media accounts. Check and manage those app permissions regularly.

- Guard Your Password Fortress: Your password is your secret weapon. Keep it strong, keep it unique, and consider adding that extra layer of protection with two-factor authentication.

* Check Your Social Media Radar: Regularly check in on your social media activity. If something does not look right, take action. It is your turf; keep it safe and sound.

Say No to Cyberbullying

When someone uses digital tools to harass, intimidate, or hurt others, that is cyberbullying. It is harmful because it can mess with your mental health and self-esteem and make your online space feel unsafe. Whether it's sending mean texts, spreading rumors, or sharing embarrassing stuff to hurt someone, all of it constitutes cyberbullying. It is not just plain disagreements that are random; rather, it is intentional and hurtful. Unfortunately, it is more common than we would think. Social media, chat apps, and gaming platforms can be its breeding grounds. Cyberbullying statistics are a wake-up call for all of us. Around 37% of teens in the U.S. report being cyberbullied. That is too many, right? So, let's make the change. If you see it happening or experience it, speak up. Block and report the people harassing you in any way; save the evidence; and talk to someone you trust about it. You are not alone in this battle. Reach out to helplines such as the National Suicide Prevention Lifeline at **1-800-273-TALK (1-800-273-8255)** or text "**HELLO**" to **741741** to connect with the Crisis Text Line. Remember, your online space should be a positive vibe zone. Let's make the change and stand up against cyberbullying! And while you report, make sure that you do not use it as a tool to purposely hurt someone's reputation; only report when you actually face cyberbullying to keep credibility in your voice.

Say you are scrolling through your feed and you spot someone getting picked on or treated unfairly. That is the moment to let your inner superhero speak up. Be the friend who stands up against the cyberbullies, the one who turns the situation around with a sprinkle of kindness. It is not just about being nice; it is about creating a vibe where everyone feels safe, respected, and welcome. Your simple act of kindness can be the game-changer that turns a negative online scene into a positive one. Intervene, offer help to the friend who is being targeted, and register a complaint against those who are harassing others.

Protect Your Personal Information Online:

When you share your personal information online, you expose yourself to various risks. One major concern is privacy invasion, as details such as your full name, address, or phone number may lead to unwanted attention or potential harm from strangers. Another risk is cyberbullying, where personal information shared online can be weaponized against you in hurtful ways. Posting explicit content or sharing intimate details may have long-lasting consequences, as it affects your reputation both online and offline. The dark side of the internet is that once you post something publicly, it goes out of your hands, and you can never take it down. Even the personal and intimate pictures that you might share with your friends or relationship partners online are not safe and may get leaked out due to any possible cause. That is the risk that you should never take, as it is going to hurt your self-esteem and reputation in many ways.

Plus, sharing your location can compromise your safety, as it might disclose where you are at any given moment. Remember, not everyone online has good intentions, so being cautious about what you share helps protect you from these risks and ensures a safer digital experience. The internet is great for learning and connecting, but there are some things you should keep to yourself.

First off, try not to use your full name everywhere online. Using a nickname or just part of your name can help protect you. Do not spill the beans on details such as your home address, phone number, or school name. Bad people exist online, so keeping these things under wraps helps keep you safe. Those who know you personally would know those details already, so there is no need to share them online.

Be careful about sharing your exact pin location. Some apps love to share where you are, and that is not always a good thing. Turn off the location-sharing feature on your Snapchat or other apps, and think twice before telling everyone where you are at all times.

And when it comes to online friends, be smart. Do not give away personal information to people you just met. It takes time to build trust, so be cautious about friend requests and private chats with people you do not know in real life. No matter how genuine they sound, there are still things that they may hide easily from you, and there is no way of knowing about them. So, it is best to keep your guards up and not let those people enter your personal life.

Follow safe online practices:

Your first line of defense in the digital world is a rock-solid password. Creating a password that is strong and unique keeps cyber attackers at bay. Whether its your phone, your laptop, your social media accounts, or your and chat apps, they must always be protected. Here are some best practices to follow:

- **Use Complex Passwords**: Create passwords that are at least 12 characters long and include a mix of uppercase and lowercase letters, numbers, and special characters. Avoid easily guessable information like birthdays or common words.

- **Do not use common passwords.** Steer clear of using common passwords such as "password," "123456," or "admin." These are the first choices for attackers.

- **Different Passwords for Each Account**: Avoid using the same password across multiple accounts. If one account is compromised, having unique passwords for each service limits the potential damage.

- **Change Passwords Periodically**: Regularly change your passwords, especially for sensitive accounts. This adds an extra layer of security and reduces the risk of prolonged unauthorized access.

- **Use Passphrases**: Consider using passphrases, such as longer combinations of words or a sentence. These can be easier to remember and still strong if they include a mix of characters.

- **Do not share passwords, even with your closest friends.** Do not share your passwords with others, even if they are close friends or family members. Each person should have their own secure credentials.

- **Use Two-Factor Authentication (2FA):** Wherever possible, enable 2FA for your accounts. This adds an extra layer of security by requiring a second form of verification in addition to your password.

- **Update all your software regularly.** Keep your operating system, antivirus software, and password manager (if applicable) up-to-date. Software updates often include security enhancements.

- **Review Account Activity**: Regularly review your account activity for any suspicious logins or activities. If you notice anything unusual, take immediate action, such as changing your password and enabling additional security measures.

Strategies For Recognizing and Avoiding Online Scams or Phishing Attempts

Suppose you receive an email claiming to be your favorite online game's support team. They urgently inform you that your account is compromised, and you must click on the provided link to secure it ASAP. Intrigued and worried about losing your gaming progress, you click the link. Little did you know, you had fallen into the trap of a phishing scheme. The link takes you to a fake website that looks exactly like your game's login page. Eager to save your account, you enter your username and password, unknowingly handing over the keys to your gaming kingdom to cyber criminals. Bam! You have just been phished. If you do not want to become a victim of this phishing, then here are some strategies to help you stay vigilant:

- **Check the sender's email address**: Verify the sender's email address, especially if the email claims to be from a reputable organization. Phishers often use email addresses that mimic legitimate ones but may have slight misspellings or variations.

- **Examine email content**: Be wary of emails with generic greetings or poor grammar or spelling errors. Legitimate organizations usually maintain a professional standard in their communications.

- **Look for red flags in URLs.** Hover over links in emails to preview the actual URL before clicking. Be cautious if the link address seems suspicious or does not match the claimed destination.

- **Verify the website's security (HTTPS)**: Make sure that websites where you enter personal information use "https://" in the URL. The "s" indicates a secure, encrypted connection.

- **Urgent or Threatening Language**: Scammers often create a sense of urgency or use threatening language to prompt immediate action. Be skeptical of emails or messages that demand urgent responses or threaten negative consequences.

- **Verify Requests for Personal Information**: Legitimate organizations typically do not request sensitive information (such as passwords or credit card numbers) via email or unsolicited messages. Verify such requests through official channels before responding.

- **Use Multi-Factor Authentication (MFA)**: Enable MFA whenever possible. Even if your login credentials are compromised, MFA adds an extra layer of security by requiring a second form of verification.

- **Keep Software and Antivirus Updated**: Regularly update your operating system, antivirus software, and applications. Security updates often include protections against known vulnerabilities.

- **Spam Filters:** Use spam filters provided by your email provider to reduce the likelihood of phishing emails reaching your inbox. Regularly check your spam folder for any legitimate emails that may have been mistakenly marked as spam.

- **Verify Email and Message Requests**: If you receive unexpected emails or messages requesting money or personal information, independently verify the request by contacting the person or organization through trusted and official channels.

- **Be skeptical of unsolicited attachments.** Avoid opening attachments or downloading files from unknown or unexpected sources. Malicious software often spreads through email attachments.

Tips For Staying Safe While Using Public Wi-Fi or Accessing Websites

While it is tempting to connect and scroll away through public Wi-Fi, those internet connections can be a bit like crowded streets where not everyone has good intentions. Unlike your private Wi-Fi at home, public ones can be less secure. That means the personal information you share online, such as passwords or messages, might be more vulnerable to cyberattacks. So, when using public Wi-Fi, be cautious.

- Use Secure Websites (HTTPS): Stick to websites that use "https://" in the URL. This makes sure that your data is encrypted during transmission and makes it more challenging for hackers to intercept and misuse your information.

- Avoid Public Computers for Sensitive Work: Public computers may have malware or keyloggers (they keep the record of the keys you have pressed on the keyboard) installed. Avoid accessing sensitive accounts or doing financial transactions on public computers.

- Use a Virtual Private Network (VPN): A VPN encrypts your internet connection, adding an extra layer of security. This is especially important when using public Wi-Fi, as it protects your data from potential eavesdroppers.

- Turn off Sharing: Disable file and printer sharing when connected to public networks. This prevents unauthorized access to your device and files.

- Update Your Software: Keep your operating system, antivirus, and applications up to date. Software updates often include security patches that protect against known vulnerabilities.

- Use Strong, Unique Passwords: Create strong passwords for your accounts and avoid using the same password across multiple sites. This prevents unauthorized access, even if one account is compromised.

- Log Out After Sessions: Always log out of your accounts, especially when using public computers. This makes sure that others cannot access your accounts after you have finished using them.

Digital Footprint and Reputation Management:

Think of your online presence as your giant resume that potential colleges, employers, and even friends might check out before considering you for admission or a job. What you post, comment on or share can leave a lasting impression, so it is absolutely important to showcase your best self. Inappropriate or questionable content can come back to haunt you, affecting college admissions, job applications, and even personal relationships. Remember, the online world is vast, but it is not always forgiving. Be careful about what you share. You are not just protecting your privacy; you are also setting yourself up for a positive and successful future. The best strategy is to keep your personal life away from public eyes and only share your professional and academic wins online.

ACTIVITY 5: TASK

Create your own personal cybersecurity guide. Design a visually appealing guide with infographics. Once you design the guide, get it printed to distribute among friends or family. You can also share the guide online on social media platforms to spread awareness. Do not forget to add the hashtag #saynotocyberbullying.

GUARDIANS

OF THE DIGITAL WORLD

6

CHAPTER 6:

HEALTHY HABITS: INSIDE AND OUT

In the hustle and bustle of our everyday lives, we all need to take a moment and reflect on how we are doing both mentally and physically. Juggling school with social commitments and personal challenges can be tough, and that is why checking in on your well-being is so important. Your mental health is just as vital as your physical well-being, and they both often go hand in hand. It is not just about surviving but also about thriving successfully. Self-care is not being selfish; it is a necessity. Nobody can take care of you better than yourself. As the wise words of Jim Rohn remind us, "Take care of your body. It is the only place you have to live." So, how do you manage stress and stay healthy? If you do not have a plan, then worry not! In this chapter, we will look into various ways to balance mental and physical health!

Stay Fit, Eat Healthy and Feel Great

The key to leveling up in any part of life is rocking the combination of physical and mental fitness. You will be like a supercharged character in a video game; you are ready to conquer any quest that comes your way. Good health is not just about flexing muscles; it is also about having a strong and resilient mind.

Why is healthy nutrition important?

A balanced and nutritious diet is extremely important for your growth, energy, and overall well-being. Focus on adding a variety of foods to your meals to get a range of nutrients. Add plenty of fruits and vegetables of different colors to get diverse vitamins and minerals. Choose whole grains such as brown rice, oats, and whole wheat for sustained energy, and opt for lean protein sources such as poultry, fish, beans, and tofu. Do not forget about dairy or fortified alternatives for calcium to support your bone health. Snack on nuts, seeds, or yogurt for healthy fats and additional nutrients. Hydration is also important, as your body cells are 97 percent water, so make sure to drink plenty of water throughout the day.

When you nourish your body with a balanced and nutritious diet, you provide it with the essential vitamins, minerals, and energy it needs to function optimally. A diet rich in fruits, vegetables, whole grains, and lean proteins supports physical growth, mental clarity, and emotional balance. It can boost your immune system and make you more resilient to fight against illnesses. With healthy eating habits, you can maintain stable energy levels throughout the day and stay focused and alert, whether you are at school taking a lecture or playing with friends afterwards. Make mindful choices about what you eat and consume on a daily basis. Here is how you can start making healthier food choices from now on:

- " Meal Prep: Set aside time each week to plan and prepare meals in advance. This could include chopping vegetables, cooking proteins, or assembling ready-to-go lunches.

- " Choose Whole Foods: Go for whole, minimally processed foods. Fresh fruits, vegetables, lean proteins, and whole grains provide essential nutrients without added sugars or unhealthy fats.

- " Snack Smart: Keep healthy snacks on hand, such as nuts, seeds, yogurt, or cut-up fruits and veggies. This helps you avoid reaching for less nutritious options when you are hungry between meals.

- " Hydrate Well: Drink plenty of water throughout the day. Sometimes, feelings of hunger can be mistaken for dehydration. Carry a reusable water bottle to stay hydrated while on the go.

- " Balance Macronutrients: Aim for a balance of carbohydrates, proteins, and fats in each meal. This combination helps keep you satisfied and provides sustained energy. Your meal must contain 45–65% carbs, 20–35% fats, and 10–35% protein.

" Quick and Nutritious Options: Look for quick and nutritious recipes that you can cook up in a short amount of time. This could be a smoothie, a salad with pre-cooked chicken, or a simple stir-fry with vegetables and lean protein.

" Healthy Grab-and-Go Choices: When eating out or grabbing food on the run, choose healthier options. Look for salads, grilled proteins, or whole-grain options on menus.

" Include Breakfast: Never skip breakfast. It kickstarts your metabolism and helps you make better food choices throughout the day. Go for whole-grain cereals, yogurt with fruit, or a smoothie for a quick and nutritious start.

Do not miss physical activity and exercise:

When you move your body, whether through sports, exercise, or even a brisk walk, you are not only building strength and endurance but also boosting your mood and reducing stress. Regular physical activity helps keep your heart healthy, maintains a healthy weight, and supports overall physical well-being. Moreover, it is a powerful tool for managing stress, anxiety, and depression, releasing those feel-good endorphins that can make a significant difference in your mental outlook. So, whether it is shooting hoops, dancing, or hitting the gym, finding activities you enjoy ensures that staying active becomes a fun and essential part of your daily routine, contributing to a healthier and happier you.

Start by finding activities you genuinely enjoy, whether they are dancing, biking, or team sports. This makes it easier for you to stick with your routine. Set realistic goals that match your fitness level and gradually increase intensity as you get stronger. Mix it up to keep things interesting; variety can prevent boredom and keep you motivated. Find a time that works for you, whether it is in the morning before school or in the evening. Consistency is key, so aim for at least 30 minutes of moderate exercise most days. Do not forget to listen to your body; rest is equally important for recovery. Whether you are into solo workouts or group activities, creating a routine that fits your lifestyle ensures that exercise becomes a positive and sustainable part of your daily life.

Cardiovascular Exercises

Cardio exercises get your heart pumping and improve your stamina. Some great options include:

- Running or jogging is a simple and effective way to boost cardiovascular health.
- Biking: Whether cycling outdoors or using a stationary bike, it is a fun and efficient cardio workout.
- Dancing is an enjoyable way to stay active while grooving to your favorite tunes.

Strength Training

Building muscle strength is essential for overall fitness. Consider:

- Bodyweight exercises: Try push-ups, squats, lunges, and planks to build strength without the need for equipment.
- Weightlifting: If you have access to weights, consider incorporating them into your routine to challenge and strengthen various muscle groups.

Flexibility and Stretching

Enhance your flexibility and prevent injuries with activities like:

- Yoga is a fantastic practice for flexibility, balance, and relaxation.
- Pilates focuses on core strength, flexibility, and overall muscle toning.
- Regular stretching: Try stretches before and after your workout to improve flexibility and reduce muscle stiffness.

Team Sports

Consider:

* Soccer is a fast-paced game that enhances endurance, coordination, and teamwork.

* Basketball is great for cardiovascular fitness, agility, and improving shooting and passing skills.

* Volleyball is a fun sport that engages multiple muscle groups and improves reflexes.

Outdoor Activities

Take advantage of the outdoors with activities like:

* Hiking is a great way to enjoy nature while providing a full-body workout.

* Biking: Explore your surroundings on a bike, combining exercise with outdoor adventure.

* Skateboarding enhances balance and coordination and is an exciting way to stay active.

There are several other activities that you can try like surfing, swimming, etc.

Connection Between Emotional Well-Being and Nutrition:

Have you ever noticed that what you eat can impact how you feel? The connection between emotional well-being and food choices is real. Nutrient-rich foods provide the brain with the right stuff to produce chemicals that make you feel good, such as serotonin and dopamine. On the other hand, loading up on sugary snacks or processed foods might give you a temporary energy boost, but it can lead to crashes and leave you feeling moody.

If you are feeling confused or worried about your diet and what you are eating, it is totally cool to talk to a pro about it. They can be a registered dietitian or nutritionist! They can help you figure out what foods are best for your body and how to eat in a way that fits your life. It is especially important during our teen years, when we are growing and changing a lot. These experts can give you the lowdown on good nutrition, sort out any worries you might have, and make sure you are making choices that keep you healthy now and in the future.

Create A Positive Relationship with Food

- Adopt Balance: Instead of thinking about foods in terms of "good" or "bad," focus on including a variety of foods in your diet. Balance is about enjoying a mix of fruits, veggies, whole grains, and proteins to ensure your body gets the nutrients it needs.

- Listen to Your Body: Tune in to what your body is telling you. Eat when you are hungry, and stop when you feel satisfied. This helps you build a healthy relationship with food by honoring your body's natural cues.

- No Calorie Stress: Let go of the stress of counting calories or comparing yourself to others. Concentrate on nourishing your body with wholesome foods, and do not get bogged down by strict rules.

- Moderation Matters: It is okay to enjoy treats; just do it in moderation. You do not have to deny yourself the foods you love; instead, find a balance that allows you to indulge without overdoing it.

- Do not skip meals: Skipping meals can mess with your energy levels and leave you feeling sluggish. Make sure to eat regularly to keep your body fueled and ready for whatever comes your way.

- Family and Friends Vibes: Sharing meals with friends and family creates positive vibes around eating. It is not just about the food; it is also about the connection and enjoyment of being together.

- " Trust Your Instincts: Trust yourself when making food choices. If something does not feel right or if you are unsure, listen to your instincts. Your body often knows what it needs.

- " Talk it out: If you ever feel confused or overwhelmed about food, do not hesitate to talk to someone you trust, like a parent or a professional. Sharing your concerns can provide valuable support and guidance.

Stress Busters and Chill-Out Skills:

Let's assume that you are facing a big week with tests, projects, and hanging out with friends. Suddenly, it is as if a storm of stress is brewing in your brain. The stuff you have to do keeps growing, and it feels a bit crazy. Sleep, your usual cozy time, becomes a bit tricky with all these thoughts buzzing around. Your happy mood starts to fade, and even studying becomes like fighting against a wave of stress. Friends and fun activities feel a bit overwhelming too. Taking care of yourself seems harder when stress is taking over. So, the big lesson? Let's dodge this stress storm whenever we can.

Let's understand stress and its effects:

Stress is a real deal, and it is totally normal to feel pressure from different areas of life. Common stressors for you are schoolwork, exams, peer relationships, family dynamics, and maybe even thinking about the future. While a bit of stress can be motivating, too much can take a toll on your mental health. It might mess with your mood, energy levels, and even sleep. Constant stress can lead to anxiety, mood swings, or even feeling down. The key is to recognize what is stressing you out, find healthy ways to cope, and talk to someone you trust about what you are going through. Whether it is a friend, family member, or counselor, sharing the load can make a huge difference in managing stress and keeping your mental health on track. Stress can have significant impacts on your physical health, and understanding these effects is crucial. Here is how stress can affect your body:

- Chronic stress can lead to high blood pressure, heart disease, and an increased risk of stroke.

- Stress can weaken your immune system, making you more susceptible to illnesses and infections.

- Stress may contribute to digestive issues like indigestion, acid reflux, or irritable bowel syndrome (IBS).

- Tense muscles due to stress can lead to headaches, back pain, and overall muscle tension.

- Stress can affect your breathing, potentially leading to shortness of breath or exacerbating respiratory conditions.

Remember, you are not alone in this, and taking care of your mental well-being is just as important as taking that next test. Here is the lowdown on spotting stress and handling it like a pro:

Check your body cues:
- Tight Muscles: If your muscles feel like they are in a knot, that could be a sign.

- Headaches or Tummy Troubles: Sometimes stress can mess with your head or stomach.

- Sleep Struggles: If you are tossing and turning, stress might be tagging along.

Watch your emotions:
- Mood Swings: If you are going from happy to grumpy in seconds, stress could be playing games.

- Feeling Overwhelmed: When everything feels like too much, it might be stress knocking on your door.

- Cannot Concentrate: If focusing is harder than usual, stress might be the culprit.

Listen to your habits:

- Eating Changes: Stress can mess with your appetite, so watch out for sudden changes.

- Nail Biting or Fidgeting: Sometimes stress comes from physical habits.

Relaxation and Stress-Relief Techniques:

You cannot control everything. It is okay to want things to go your way, but sometimes life has its own plans. Focus on what you can control, and let go of the rest.

Deep Breathing: Find a quiet space and sit or lie down comfortably. Inhale deeply through your nose to allow your lungs to fill with air. Hold your breath for a few seconds and exhale slowly through your mouth, imagining you are releasing all the stress and tension. Repeat this process for several minutes.

Progressive Muscle Relaxation (PMR): Start by tensing and then slowly releasing each muscle group, starting from your toes and working your way up to your head. Tense each muscle group for about 5–10 seconds and then release, paying attention to the sensations of tension and relaxation.

Guided Imagery: Close your eyes and imagine yourself in a peaceful place, such as a beach, forest ,or meadow. Focus on the details—the sound of waves, the rustling of leaves, or the warmth of the sun. Engage all your senses in this mental escape that allows your mind to focus on positive and calming imagery.

Mindfulness Meditation: Sit comfortably and focus on your breath. Be aware of each inhale and exhale, observing the sensations without judgment. If your mind starts to wander, gently bring it back to your breath.

Yoga: Practice simple yoga poses or sequences that encourage relaxation. The combination of gentle movements, stretching, and focused breathing can help calm the mind and relax the body.

Listening to Music: Create a playlist of calming music that you enjoy. Close your eyes and focus on the music that allows it to soothe your mind and transport you to a more peaceful state.

Journaling: Write down your thoughts and feelings in a journal. Reflect on positive aspects of your day or express gratitude. Putting your thoughts on paper can help you process emotions and gain perspective.

Nature Walks: Take a leisurely walk in a natural setting, such as a park or a trail. Pay attention to the sights, sounds, and smells around you, and let nature's calming influence work its magic.

Experiment with these techniques and find what works best for you. It is perfectly okay to mix and match or adapt them to suit your preferences.

Strategies For Creating a Calm and Soothing Environment to Unwind and Relax

A calm and soothing environment is necessary for unwinding and relaxing. Here are some strategies to turn your living space into a soothing environment:

- Choose Soft Colors: Try soft, neutral colors like blues, greens, or earth tones. These colors are known for promoting a sense of calm and relaxation. Avoid overly bright or stimulating colors.

- Comfortable Furniture: Whether it is a cozy chair, a soft blanket, or a plush rug, make sure your space is designed for comfort.

- Good Lighting: Use soft, warm lighting instead of harsh, bright lights. Consider adding floor or table lamps with adjustable brightness to create a more soothing atmosphere.

- Natural Elements: Connect with elements of nature, such as plants, flowers, or natural materials such as wood. Nature has a calming effect and can help create a connection to the outdoors.

- Declutter: Keep your space tidy and organized. Clutter can contribute to a feeling of chaos and stress. Simplify your surroundings to promote a sense of calm.

- Aromatherapy: Use essential oils or scented candles to introduce calming scents into your space. Scents such as lavender, chamomile, and eucalyptus are known for their relaxing properties.

- Soft Textures: Use soft textures through cushions, throws, or rugs. The tactile sensation of soft materials can enhance the comfort and coziness of your space.

- Personal Touch: Add personal items that bring you joy and relaxation, such as photographs, artwork, or sentimental objects. These can create a sense of connection and happiness.

- Noise Control: Minimize external noises that can disrupt your peace. Consider using earplugs, white noise machines, or calming music to drown out unwanted sounds.

- Technology-Free Zone: Create a space that is free from the distractions of technology. Keep your phone, computer, and other electronic devices away to promote a break from the digital world.

- Comfortable Temperature: Maintain a comfortable temperature in the room. Adjust the heating or cooling to ensure the space is neither too hot nor too cold for relaxation.

- Reading Nook or Meditation Space: Designate a specific area for activities such as reading, meditation, or mindfulness exercises. Having a dedicated space for these practices can help signal to your brain that it is time to unwind.

Balancing Activities for Mental Health:

Whether it is art, jamming out, writing, sports, or whatever rocks your boat, these things let you dive into what you love. Doing your hobbies gives you a break, lets you explore what you are into, and maybe even reveals some cool talents you did not know you had. Plus, it makes you feel good about yourself and boosts your confidence. When life gets stressful, these hobbies are your go-to moves; they help you kick back, be present, and forget about the drama.

Let's talk about the two most valuable players in your mental health: sleep and relaxing time. Seriously, getting enough Zs and downtime is a secret weapon against stress and keeping your whole vibe in check. Your body and brain need that sleep to recover and recharge. Lack of sleep messes with your mood, makes stress feel 100 times worse, and can even mess with your memory and focus. So, make your bed your best friend, aim for those 8 hours, and do not underestimate the power of Netflix and naps. It is not just about catching Zs; it is about being the boss of your stress and staying on top of your game.

Keeping Your Mind in Top Shape:

Flexing those brain muscles is as crucial as hitting the gym for a killer workout. Seriously, keeping your mind sharp is not just for acing exams; it is a game-changer for life. When you challenge your brain with puzzles, reading, or even trying new stuff, you are basically giving it a power-up. A sharp mind helps you solve problems, be creative, and tackle anything life throws your way. Plus, it is a secret weapon for personal growth, making you a smarter, more confident version of yourself. Ready to boost your brainpower? Here are some awesome activities and practices to keep your mental game strong:

" Read for Fun: Dive into books that interest you. Whether it is fiction, non-fiction, or graphic novels, reading enhances vocabulary, improves focus, and sparks creativity.

- Puzzles and Brain Games: Solve puzzles, crosswords, or try brain games. They are a workout for your brain, improving problem-solving skills and memory.

- Learn a New Skill: Challenge yourself to pick up a new hobby or skill, be it coding, playing an instrument, or even cooking. Learning new things builds new connections in your brain.

- Mindful Meditation: Practice mindfulness and meditation to calm the mind. It is a mental reset that reduces stress, improves focus, and boosts overall well-being.

- Creative Writing: Express yourself through writing. Whether it is keeping a journal, writing stories, or writing poetry, it enhances language skills and encourages creativity.

- Play Strategy Games: Engage in strategy games like chess or strategy-based video games. They sharpen your critical thinking and decision-making skills.

- Physical Exercise: Believe it or not, hitting the gym or going for a jog is not just for the body; it is fantastic for the brain too. Exercise improves memory and concentration.

- Join a Debate Club: Express your opinions, listen to others, and engage in debates. It hones your communication skills, critical thinking, and understanding of different perspectives.

- Attend Workshops or Classes: Participate in workshops or classes that interest you. Whether it is science, art, or technology, expanding your knowledge is a brain booster.

- Socialize and Connect: Hang out with friends, join clubs, or get involved in social activities. Socializing is not just fun; it enhances your emotional intelligence and communication skills.

Emotional intelligence and resilience:

When emotional stress hits, self-care is your power-up move. It is not just the occasional bubble bath or a Netflix binge; it is a daily commitment to your mental well-being. Do not be shy about looking for support from your squad, whether it is from friends, family, or someone you trust. You are not alone in this adventure. Prioritize self-care like it is a homework assignment for your heart, and remember, it is okay to lean on others when the going gets tough.

Develop your EI:

Emotional intelligence (EI) is a powerful set of tools for understanding and managing your own emotions and those of others. It involves being aware of your feelings, having the ability to express them appropriately, and understanding how emotions can influence your thoughts and actions. But it goes beyond that; emotional intelligence also includes being attuned to other people's emotions, empathizing with them, and navigating social situations effectively. There are four main components of emotional intelligence:

- Self-awareness: recognize and understand your own emotions. This involves being in tune with how you feel and why.

- Self-regulation: Manage and control your emotions, especially in challenging situations. It is about staying calm under pressure and not letting strong emotions drive impulsive actions.

- Social awareness: being aware of others' emotions and understanding the dynamics of social situations. This involves empathy—putting yourself in someone else's shoes to understand their feelings.

- Relationship management: Use your emotional awareness to navigate social interactions successfully. This means effective communication, conflict resolution, and building positive relationships.

Emotional intelligence helps you handle stress, build strong relationships, and make better decisions.

Handling Emotions, Building Resilience and Bouncing Back from Challenges

You can handle your emotions and bounce back from challenges using a few effective techniques:

- Feel Your Feels: It is okay to feel a mix of emotions. Allow yourself to acknowledge and understand what you are feeling. Do not shove them aside; let them flow.

- Mindful Breathing: When things get intense, take a breather. Practice mindful breathing, inhale the good vibes, and exhale the stress.

- Talk it out: Do not keep everything bottled up. Share your feelings with someone you trust—friends, family, or a mentor. Talking it out can lighten the emotional load.

- Positive Self-Talk: Be your own cheerleader. Instead of focusing on what went wrong, think about what you have learned and how you can grow from challenges. Positive self-talk is your daily pep talk.

- Problem-Solving Skills: Break down challenges into smaller parts and tackle them one step at a time. Developing problem-solving skills is your superhero utility belt for real-life situations.

- Learn from Setbacks: See setbacks as setups for comebacks. Every challenge is a chance to learn and grow.

- Healthy Coping Mechanisms: Find healthy ways to cope with stress, whether it is through art, music, sports, or even a good laugh. Healthy coping mechanisms keep your mental and emotional well-being in check.

- Build a Support System: Be with a supportive squad. Friends, family or mentors can be your backup when facing challenges. Share your experiences and lean on your support system.

- Set realistic goals: have goals, but make them achievable. Small victories add up, and achieving them boosts your confidence, making you more resilient.

- Flexibility and Adaptability: Life does not always go as planned, and that is okay. Be flexible and adapt to changes. It is being a ninja, quick on your feet, and ready for anything.

- Focus on What You Can Control: Some things are out of your control. Instead of stressing about them, concentrate on what you can control. It is a game-changer for resilience.

- Practice self-care: Take care of yourself physically and mentally. Regular exercise, proper sleep, and self-care rituals are rituals that keep you strong and resilient.

Healthy Habits for Brain Health:

Your squad, friendships, and relationships are not just there for Instagram pictures they play a massive role in keeping your mental health on point. A solid support system is your superhero team for your emotions. Positive connections provide a space to share your feelings, get advice, and feel understood. Good friendships shield against stress and boost your overall mood. Your brain is the captain of your spaceship, and keeping it in tip-top shape is key to a smooth ride through life. Check out these lifestyle habits that contribute to maintaining a healthy brain and awesome mental well-being:

- Eat Brain-Boosting Foods: Fuel your brain with goodness. Omega-3 fatty acids (found in fish), fruits, veggies, and whole grains are brain snacks that keep you sharp.

- Stay Hydrated: Water is not just for your body; it is a brain elixir. Stay hydrated, and your brain will thank you for staying focused and alert.

- Exercise Your Body and Mind: Move that body! Exercise is not just for muscles; it is a brain workout too. And do not forget to exercise your mind; puzzles, reading, and learning new things are brain push-ups.

- Limit Screen Time: Screens are cool, but too much screen time can mess with your brain vibes. Take breaks, look away, and give your eyes and brain a rest.

- Connect with Nature: Nature is a spa day for your brain. Whether it is a walk in the park or just chilling under a tree, spending time in nature boosts your mood and brainpower.

- Practice stress management: Stress is kryptonite for your brain. Practice stress-busting techniques like deep breathing, mindfulness, or talking to a friend.

- Maintain Social Connections: Your pals are brain allies. Positive social connections keep your mind happy and healthy. Hang out, share laughs, and be there for each other.

- Practice Gratitude: Be thankful for the good stuff in your life. Practicing gratitude rewires your brain to focus on the positive, making you feel happier.

- Make a Routine: Your brain loves routines. Set a daily schedule; it helps your brain know what to expect and reduces stress.

- Get creative: Express yourself! Whether it is through art, music, or writing, creativity is a brain party. It sparks joy and keeps your mind agile.

A Supportive Environment for Mental and Emotional Wellness

Create a welcoming space for yourself amidst life's chaos for your mental and emotional wellness. Open up and encourage honest communication with friends, family, or mentors to foster a supportive atmosphere. Be in positive relationships that act like sunshine for your soul. Designate safe spaces, whether it is your room, a cozy nook, or a quiet spot in nature, where you can unwind and be yourself. Express your emotions creatively through art, writing, or music, turning your feelings into a masterpiece. Follow healthy habits like exercise, good sleep, and nutritious eating, as a healthy body supports a healthy mind. Practice mindfulness or relaxation techniques with friends or family to create a shared experience and promote calm.

Celebrate achievements, big or small, for positive reinforcement that boosts confidence and happiness. Face challenges as a team, whether they're school projects or personal goals. Learn about mental health together, sharing resources that promote understanding and awareness. Respect personal space and boundaries, acknowledging that everyone needs their own bubble sometimes. Encourage help-seeking as a strength, whether talking to someone or seeking professional support. Lastly, promote an inclusive environment that accepts diversity, recognizing that everyone's uniqueness adds flavor to your supportive community.

ACTIVITY 6: A MEAL PLAN

Create your own daily or weekly meal plan. Add a list of your recipes and groceries, according to the given template:

weekly meal plan

from _____ to _____

grocery list

| monday |
| tuesday |
| wednesday |
| thursday |
| friday |
| saturday |
| sunday |

notes:

HARMONY
OF HEALTH

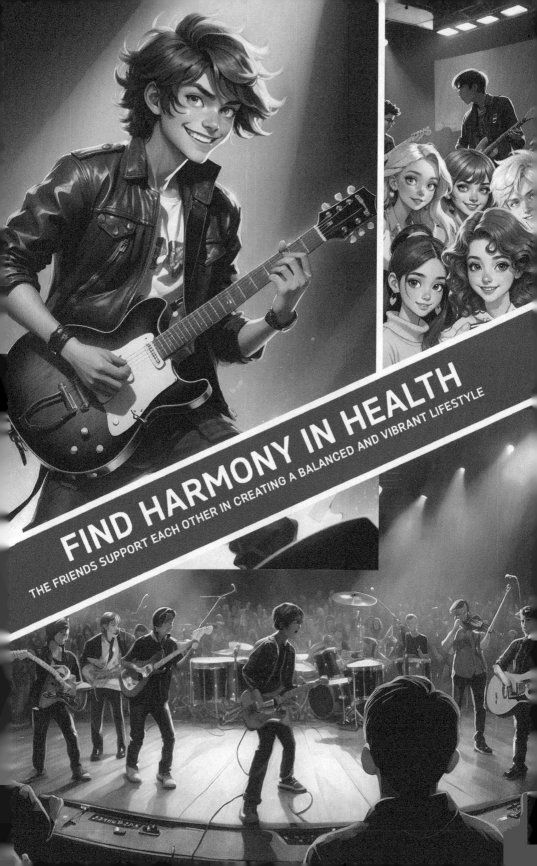

FIND HARMONY IN HEALTH

THE FRIENDS SUPPORT EACH OTHER IN CREATING A BALANCED AND VIBRANT LIFESTYLE

7

CHAPTER 7:

CAREER QUEST: JOBS, HUSTLES AND DREAMING BIG

The pressure to choose the right subjects and make informed decisions can be daunting at this age ,and it is completely normal to feel confused and stuck. But do not worry, because I have got you covered! In this chapter, we will explore some of the best techniques to guide you through this important phase of your life. From helping you make informed decisions about the career you want to pursue to providing insights on exploring different career paths, here we will explore all the tools to empower you. We will look into the art of crafting compelling resumes and acing interviews, preparing you for the professional world that awaits. So, buckle up and get ready for self-discovery and career preparation!

Identifying Your Interests and Career Options:

Figuring out what you are into and what you are good at can be a bit tricky, especially when thinking about future careers. One way to start is by thinking about the things that really make you excited and happy. It could be hobbies, school subjects, or stuff you do outside of class. Try making a list or keeping a journal to spot any patterns. There are great tools out there that can help too, such as career aptitude tests and personality quizzes. They can give you ideas about careers that match your strengths and interests. Your school's guidance counselor can hook you up with these tests, so do not hesitate to ask!

Have you ever thought about exploring different careers hands-on? Going to career fairs, trying out internships, or talking with professionals in different fields can give you a taste of what's out there. There are also online platforms where you can virtually shadow someone's job, which is pretty cool. And here is a tip: don't be shy about reaching out to people in careers you find interesting. Teachers, family friends, or pros on social media can be great mentors. They can share their experiences and give you the inside scoop on what their jobs are really like.

"Let's Explore Your Interests!" Questionnaire

Are you feeling a bit lost when it comes to your interests and not quite sure where to steer your ship? No worries! Have you ever wondered what truly captivates your attention and sparks your curiosity? If you find yourself drawing a blank, fret not! I have prepared a questionnaire that will help peel the layers of your interests.

Q What subjects or activities do you enjoy at school or in your free time? (e.g., math, art, sports, coding, music)

_____

_____

Q If you could spend a day doing anything you love without worrying about time or money, what would it be?

_____

_____

Q Are there certain hobbies or activities that make you lose track of time when you are doing them?

_____

_____

Q Imagine your dream job; what would you be doing, and what kind of environment would you be in?

_____

_____

Q Which school subjects or topics do you find most intriguing or exciting?

_____

_____

Q What skills do your friends and family often compliment you on? (e.g., communication, problem-solving, creativity)

_____

_____

Q If you had to pick one cause or issue in the world to work on, what would it be? (e.g., environment, social justice, health)

_____

_____

Q Do you enjoy working independently, in a team, or a mix of both?

_____

_____

Q What kind of books, movies, or documentaries do you find most captivating?

_____

_____

Q Think about a problem you'd love to solve in the world. What is it, and how would you approach it?

_____

_____

Q Consider your favorite role models or people you look up to; what about their careers or achievements inspires you?

_____

_____

Q When you picture yourself in the future, what kind of lifestyle and work-life balance do you envision?

_____

_____

The answer to the above questions will help you gain a deeper understanding of your aims and interest.

Researching career options:

In this age of endless possibilities, exploring various career paths is the key to finding what truly lights up your passion. In-depth and detailed research opens doors to worlds you might not have considered while making informed decisions about your future. When you learn about different industries, you gain the power of adaptability, which is crucial in a world where careers can be as dynamic as your favorite video game levels. Check out these resources and opportunities to gain valuable insights:

Online Career Platforms: Websites such as LinkedIn, Indeed, and Glassdoor provide a wealth of information about different careers, job roles, required qualifications, and even real employee reviews.

Virtual Job Fairs: Attend virtual job fairs or career expos where you can interact with professionals from various industries, learn about job opportunities, and get a feel for different workplaces.

Informational Interviews: Reach out to professionals in your desired field for informational interviews. This informal discussion allows you to learn about their experiences, challenges, and the day-to-day aspects of their job.

Job Shadowing and Internships: Shadowing or interning in a specific role lets you immerse yourself in the work environment, observe daily tasks, and understand the industry firsthand.

Books, Documentaries, and Podcasts: Dive into books, documentaries, and podcasts related to specific careers. They offer valuable insights, success stories, and sometimes a reality check about different industries.

School Career Counselors: Your school's career counselors are career wizards. Schedule appointments to discuss your interests with them, get guidance, and explore potential career paths tailored to your strengths and goals. There is no harm in talking to someone and gaining more knowledge. The more you know, the better it is for decision-making.

Industry-Specific Events: Attend industry-specific events, workshops, or conferences. These gatherings often feature experts and professionals sharing their experiences, industry trends, and networking opportunities.

Online Courses and Certifications: Explore platforms such as Coursera, Udemy, or LinkedIn Learning as they offer courses and certifications that give you a taste of specific skills required in different careers.

Goal Setting and Career Planning:

Start by tapping into your interests and passions. What makes you excited and curious? Reflect on your strengths and skills; they are your trusted tools for the process ahead. Break down your aspirations into achievable steps. Consider exploring careers that align with your interests and values, creating a roadmap tailored to your unique talents. Stay open to evolving goals; it is okay to pivot as you discover more about yourself.

Short-term plans are the quests you tackle today: acing that test, joining that football team or club, or gaining a new skill. They keep you on track and boost your confidence. Long-term plans are the grand quest. They give your journey purpose and direction. By balancing both, you create a roadmap for success. Short-term wins fuel your motivation, while long-term visions guide your choices. The following strategies can help you create a personalized roadmap:

- Clearly outline your short-term and long-term career goals. What do you want to achieve in the next year? In the next five years?

- Dive deep into your chosen career path. Understand the required qualifications, skills, and experiences. What are the current trends and future prospects?

- Break down the skills needed for your chosen career. Assess your current skill set and identify areas for improvement.

- Create specific, measurable, and time-bound milestones. These can include completing a course, gaining internship experience, or acquiring a certification.

- Connect with professionals in your field of interest. Attend networking events, join online forums, and look for mentorship. Building relationships can open doors to opportunities.

- Look for internships, part-time jobs, or volunteer opportunities. Hands-on experience is gold on your resume and gives you a taste of the real work world.

- Stay curious and invest in continuous learning. Attend workshops and webinars or take online courses to stay updated on industry trends.

- Do not be afraid to look for feedback from mentors, professionals, or teachers. Constructive feedback helps you grow and refine your action plan.

- Be open to adjusting your plan as you gain new insights. The career landscape may evolve, and flexibility is your secret weapon.

- Regularly assess your progress against your milestones. What is working well? Where can you make improvements? Adjust your plan accordingly.

Resume Building and Interview Skills:

Your resume is your personal highlight reel that showcases all the great stuff you have done and the skills you have gained. A good resume is your golden ticket to opening doors for opportunities. It is the first impression you make on potential employers, and it can speak volumes about your capabilities and achievements. A well-crafted resume not only reflects your academic achievements but also highlights your extracurricular activities, volunteer work, and any part-time jobs or internships you have tackled. It is not just a list of your experiences, but a chance to shine and stand out from the crowd. So, polish up your resume, make it a true reflection of your skills and experiences, and let it be the key to unlocking exciting opportunities on your journey to success! The components that make a strong and compelling resume include:

* Contact Info: Put your name, phone number, email, and maybe your LinkedIn profile.

* Objective or Summary: A short statement about your career goals and what you are good at.

* Education: Tell them where you go to school, when you will graduate, your GPA if it is good, and any cool classes or awards.

* Skills: List what you are good at, both technical stuff (computer skills) and people skills (being a team player).

* Work Experience: Talk about any jobs or volunteer work you have done. Say what you did and what you achieved.

* Extracurricular Activities: Mention clubs, sports, or community service you are involved in, especially if you have taken a leadership role.

* Projects: If you have worked on school projects or personal stuff, share a bit about them.

* Achievements and Awards: Put down any awards or recognition you have gotten.

* Certifications and Courses: If you have finished any courses or got certifications, let them know.

* References: If you have someone who can vouch for you, add them. But ask first!

Keep it neat and easy to read with a regular font. Be consistent with how you format things. You can also add a section about your hobbies, languages you know, or memberships you have.

Tips for highlighting skills, experiences, and achievements on a resume?

If you want your resume to leave a good impression on every person who views it, then:

* **Use Action Verbs:** Start each bullet point with strong action verbs like "managed," "created," or "achieved" to make your experiences more impactful.

* **Quantify Achievements**: Whenever possible, include numbers to quantify your achievements. For instance, "increased sales by 20%" or "completed 50 volunteer hours."

* **Tailor to the Job**: Customize your resume for each job application. Highlight the skills and experiences most relevant to the specific role you are applying for.

* **Focus on Results**: Instead of just listing your duties, emphasize the outcomes of your work. What positive impact did you have?

* **Prioritize Relevant Skills**: Place the most important and relevant skills at the top of your skills section. This ensures they catch the employer's attention.

* **Show your growth**: If you have been in a role for a while, showcase how you have grown or taken on more responsibilities over time.

* **Use the right and relevant keywords**: Add keywords from the job description to your resume. Many companies use applicant tracking systems (ATS) that scan for specific words.

* **Include Soft Skills**: Do not forget to highlight soft skills such as communication, teamwork, and problem-solving. They are just as important as technical skills.

* **Add your story**: Arrange your experiences and achievements in a way that tells a story about your professional journey. This helps the reader understand your career narrative.

* **Highlight Relevant Projects:** If you have worked on significant projects, give them a dedicated section. Describe your role, the project's goals, and the outcomes.

Mastering Interview Techniques:

Once your resume creates a lasting impression, you are then called for an interview, which is another big challenge. It requires confidence and self-belief to let employers believe in your capabilities. The more you practice, the stronger you become at communicating with the interviewers. Practice with a friend or family member, or even in front of a mirror. This helps build confidence and sharpen your responses. When you are well-prepared, nerves take a backseat, and you can showcase your best self. Let's go through some of the most common interview questions that you may come across and their effective answers to prepare you for the ultimate test:

Tell Me About Yourself:

You can say something along the lines of "I am a problem-solving enthusiast with a passion for (specific interest or skill). Whether it is tackling complex math problems or organizing events, I love a good challenge."

Why should we hire you?

Try something like, "You should hire me because I bring a mix of creativity and determination. My knack for a specific skill has led to an achievement or project, and I'm excited to bring that same energy to your team."

What are your strengths and weaknesses?

You can answer by saying, "One of my strengths is attention to detail, which I honed during (mention relevant experience). As for weaknesses, I am working on improving my public speaking skills by joining the school club or activity."

Describe a challenge you overcame:
Say something like, "In a school project, we faced a tight deadline. I took the lead and organized tasks, and we not only met the deadline but also received positive outcomes or feedback."

Where do you see yourself in 5 years?
"In five years, I see myself taking on more responsibilities and contributing to a specific aspect of the company. I am excited about the opportunity to grow professionally within your dynamic team."

Why do you want this job?
"Your company's commitment to (mention a value or initiative) aligns perfectly with my own values. I'm excited about the chance to contribute my specific skill to a team that values innovation."

Can You Share a Teamwork Experience?
"During a group project, my role was (certain role), and our collaboration resulted in (positive outcome, grade, or achievement). Teamwork brings out the best in me, and I'm eager to bring that spirit to your team."

How do you handle stress or pressure?
"I handle stress by breaking tasks into manageable parts and focusing on solutions. For instance, during exams, I create a study schedule and prioritize topics. It helps me stay calm and perform at my best."

Tell Me About a Time You Demonstrated Leadership:
"I led a project or activity, coordinating tasks and ensuring everyone's strengths were utilized. Our success was evident when we shared a positive outcome."

What are your interests or hobbies?
"I love any interest or hobby because it sharpens my relevant skill. For instance, my interest in any hobby has enhanced my communication or teamwork skills, which I believe would benefit your team."

Show Them Your Confidence, Professionalism and Enthusiasm

Research the company, understand the job role, and anticipate common interview questions. The more you know, the more confident and prepared you will feel. Rehearse your answers to common questions we discussed with a friend or family member. Practice boosts confidence and helps you articulate your thoughts clearly.

During the interview, keep good posture—do not slouch, make eye contact, and offer a firm handshake. Non-verbal cues speak volumes about your confidence and professionalism. Wear appropriate and formal attire for the interview. Dressing professionally not only shows respect but also boosts your own confidence.

Enunciate your words clearly and speak at a moderate pace. This exudes confidence and makes sure that your enthusiasm comes across clearly. Express why you are excited about the opportunity and ask thoughtful questions about the company culture and expectations.

When discussing your accomplishments, be proud but humble. Showcase how your skills and experiences align with the job requirements without sounding boastful. Listen attentively to the interviewer's questions and respond thoughtfully. This shows respect, professionalism, and your ability to engage in meaningful conversation.

Frame your responses in a positive light. Instead of saying what you cannot do, focus on what you have learned or how eager you are to acquire new skills. Approach the interview with a positive mindset. Enthusiasm is contagious, and a positive attitude can leave a lasting impression. Be yourself. Authenticity builds trust, and interviewers appreciate genuine candidates. Do not be afraid to show your personality along with your professionalism.

It is normal to feel nervous, but do not let it overwhelm you. Take deep breaths, smile, and remember that the interviewer wants to get to know you. Send a thank-you email expressing gratitude for the opportunity. Reiterate your enthusiasm for the position and briefly mention why you believe you are a strong fit.

Professional Communication and Etiquette:

These etiquettes are the magic spells that create an environment of professionalism, making you stand out in the interview quest. Here is how you can effectively communicate your qualifications and suitability for a job:

Highlight your education:

"With a solid foundation in (mention relevant coursework or degree), I bring a strong academic background that equips me for success in this role."

Showcase your skills:

"My proficiency in (specific skills, e.g., communication, teamwork, problem-solving) has been honed through (mention relevant experiences) and positions me as a valuable asset for your team."

Emphasize Your Experience:

"Having successfully navigated (mention specific project or job), I have gained practical experience in (key responsibilities) and developed a keen understanding of (industry/field)."

Quantify Your Achievements:

"In my previous role, I increased (specific metric, e.g., sales, efficiency) by (percentage) through (describe actions taken). These results showcase my ability to drive positive outcomes."

Link your skills to the job:

"My proficiency in (specific software or tool mentioned in the job description) positions me to seamlessly integrate into your team and contribute from day one."

Demonstrate Your Level of Adaptability:
"I perform best in dynamic settings, as demonstrated by my ability to (name a difficult task or project) under pressure. This adaptability aligns with the fast-paced nature of your industry."

Express Your Enthusiasm:
"I am particularly excited about the opportunity to contribute my passion for (specific aspect of the job or industry) and bring fresh perspectives to your team."

Tell them how you align with company values:
"I am drawn to your company's commitment to (mention a specific value or initiative), and I am eager to contribute my skills and enthusiasm to support these goals."

After the interview, send a professional and courteous follow-up message. Express your gratitude for the opportunity, reiterate your enthusiasm for the position, and briefly mention what excites you about contributing to the team. This follow-up is not just a formality; it is your chance to leave a lasting impression and show that you appreciate the interviewer's time. So, do not forget to hit "send" on that virtual thank-you scroll and leave a positive mark as you await the next chapter in your professional journey!

Work Ethic and Professionalism in the Workplace:

In the workplace, a strong work ethic and professionalism define your character and shape your success story. Your work ethic shows your commitment to hard work, dedication, and willingness to go above and beyond. Pair this with professionalism to exhibit a positive attitude, show respect towards colleagues, and stick to workplace norms. Demonstrating a strong work ethic and professionalism not only enhances your individual performance but also contributes to a positive and collaborative work environment.

What Is Work Ethics?

A strong work ethic is the backbone of success in the workplace. It is the commitment to putting in your best effort, consistently accepting challenges, and persevering through setbacks. Having a strong work ethic means not just meeting expectations but exceeding them, taking initiative, and being accountable for your responsibilities. It is essential in the workplace because it builds trust, reliability, and a positive reputation. Employers value individuals who demonstrate a strong work ethic as they contribute to a productive and efficient work environment. It is the engine that propels your professional journey forward, earning you respect from colleagues and superiors and paving the way for career growth.

- Show up when you are supposed to. It proves you respect everyone's time and can be relied upon.

- Step up and lend a hand, especially when things get busy. It shows you are committed to the team's success.

- Share your career goals and let others know you want to take on more responsibilities. It signals your commitment to growing in your role.

- Believe in your abilities and be ready to take on challenges. It demonstrates your commitment to giving your best to the team.

- Collaborate effectively, share what you know, and support team goals. It shows you are committed to the team's success over your personal achievements.

- Look for input on your performance. It proves your commitment to getting better and contributing your best work.

- Welcome feedback from your colleagues. It shows your commitment to learning and creating a positive work environment.

- Take charge of projects, motivate others, and show initiative. It reveals your commitment to drive positive change and lead by example.

- Recognize and appreciate your colleagues' efforts. It reflects your commitment to valuing everyone's contributions.

Challenges at the workplace are inevitable, but your response to them defines your professionalism. When faced with a challenge or conflict, approach it calmly and objectively. Communication is your golden tool; express your concerns or viewpoints respectfully and listen to others' perspectives. If the issue persists, seek guidance from a supervisor or HR professional. Remember, teamwork is all about collaboration, so be open to compromise and find common ground. In situations of disagreement, maintain your composure, avoid confrontations, and focus on finding constructive solutions.

Continuous learning and growth:

In today's dynamic work landscape, where change is constant, those who embrace learning stay ahead of the curve. Learning new skills, reskilling, and upskilling not only make you more adaptable but also position you as an invaluable asset in any workplace. It means equipping yourself with a versatile tool kit that empowers you to tackle challenges and excel in various aspects of your professional life.

Constantly look for new workshops, online courses, or local programs that align with your interests and career goals. Attend industry events or seminars to broaden your knowledge and network with professionals. Do not be shy about expressing your eagerness to learn and asking for advice. Mentorship is a powerful force that can illuminate your path to success, offering wisdom and encouragement as you navigate the twists and turns of your professional adventure.

ACTIVITY 7: CONDUCT AN INTERVIEW

Connect with some professionals from the career field you are interested in. Prepare questions about their job and career path, then conduct an interview to learn from their experience. Write down their responses or record this interview with their permission, then share with your friends and discuss to make notes and learn new things.

INTERVIEW PREPS

8

CHAPTER 8:

HOME SURVIVAL SKILLS: COOKING, CLEANING AND BEYOND

Home survival skills such as cooking, cleaning, and other household tasks are not simply chores that you run away from; they are essential life skills that contribute to your overall well-being and independence. When you are able to prepare your own meals, you become self-sufficient. Likewise, keeping a clean and organized living space creates a positive and hygienic environment for you. These skills not only make you self-reliant but also instill a sense of responsibility and resourcefulness. So, its about time to learn these skills and make them a part of our routine.

Basic Cooking Skills and Meal Planning

The journey to becoming a newbie cook begins with making simple and nutritious meals. Start with recipes that have a handful of ingredients and uncomplicated steps. Experiment with easy-to follow recipes for salads, stir-fries, or pasta dishes. Focus on mastering basic skills like how to chop, dice, and mince safely. Add a variety of colorful vegetables, lean proteins, and whole grains to ensure a balanced meal. Online platforms, cookbooks, or even cooking classes can be excellent resources to guide you. As you gradually build your skills, you will not only nourish your body with wholesome meals but also discover the joy of creating food that is both delicious and nutritious.

Always start by washing your hands thoroughly before handling any food. Familiarize yourself with the proper use and care of kitchen equipment, ensuring that knives and appliances are used safely. Be mindful of cross-contamination by separating raw meats from other ingredients. Keep your cooking area clean and organized to prevent accidents. Understanding these principles not only protects your health but also sets the stage for a pleasant cooking experience.

Meal Planning and Preparation

When you plan your meals, you are more likely to include a variety of fruits, vegetables, proteins, and whole grains, making sure that your body gets the nutrients it needs. It also helps you avoid the temptation of less healthy, quick options, contributing to better eating habits and overall well-being. Plus, with a plan in place, you can make grocery shopping more efficient and reduce food waste, making your journey toward a healthier lifestyle more achievable.

First, focus on balanced meals by including a mix of veggies, fruits, lean proteins, and whole grains. Second, plan meals that share ingredients to reduce waste and save money. Buying in bulk for staples such as rice or beans can be cost-effective. Choose simple recipes that do not require a lot of time or complex ingredients. Quick and nutritious options can be just as tasty. Fourth, prep ingredients in advance when you have time, making cooking during the week faster. Finally, do not forget about snacks; keep healthy options such as cut-up veggies or yogurt on hand to curb cravings without reaching for less nutritious choices. With these strategies, you are not just planning meals; you are creating a pathway to a healthier, budget-friendly and time-efficient lifestyle

Tips for grocery shopping and stocking a kitchen for meal preparation:

- Before you go to the store, think about what meals you want to make. Make a list of the things you need.

- Decide how much money you can spend and try to stay within that limit. This helps you spend wisely.

- Look for fresh fruits, veggies, meats, and dairy along the outer edges of the store. These are usually healthier choices.

- Take a moment to read the labels on packaged foods. Choose items with less sugar, fat, and salt.

- For things like rice or pasta, consider buying a lot at once. It can be cheaper, and you will always have some at home.

- Try different fruits, veggies, and proteins to make your meals interesting and good for you.

- Do not forget about frozen or canned fruits and veggies. They are easy to use and can be just as healthy as fresh ones.

- See if anything you like is on sale. It can help you save money while still getting what you need.

- Look at when food expires so you know when to use it. This stops you from wasting food and helps you plan your meals.

- Sometimes, it is okay to buy things that are already prepared, like pre-cut veggies or cooked chicken, to save time.

- Make sure your kitchen has basics like oil, spices, and condiments. They make your food taste better.

You can use the following grocery list template to organize your list of groceries before going to the store.

SHOPPING LIST

PANTRY ITEMS

- [ ]
- [ ]
- [ ]
- [ ]

- [ ]
- [ ]
- [ ]
- [ ]

FRUIT & VEGETABLES

- [ ]
- [ ]
- [ ]
- [ ]

- [ ]
- [ ]
- [ ]
- [ ]

MEAT & SEAFOOD

- [ ]
- [ ]
- [ ]
- [ ]

- [ ]
- [ ]
- [ ]
- [ ]

HOME SUPPLIES

- [ ]
- [ ]
- [ ]
- [ ]

- [ ]
- [ ]
- [ ]
- [ ]

Cooking Techniques and Recipes:

Trying out different ingredients and flavors in the kitchen is a fun adventure while cooking. Do not be scared to mix things up and see what you like. The more you try new stuff, the more you learn, and soon you will feel super sure about your cooking abilities. Some cooking techniques that you should definitely try are:

- **Sautéing**: With sautéing, you quickly cook things in a little bit of oil on medium to high heat. It is great for cooking veggies or meats quickly. Just keep the pan hot and keep tossing the ingredients for even cooking.

- **Baking**: Baking is used to cook stuff in the oven using dry heat. It is perfect for making cookies, cakes, casseroles, or roasting meats. Make sure to warm up the oven first and follow the recipe for the right measurements and time.

- **Boiling**: In boiling, you cook things in hot water until they are fully done. We do this a lot for pasta, eggs, and veggies. Add some salt to the water for extra flavor, and make sure not to overcook things.

- **Grilling**: Grilling is cooking over an open flame, such as a barbecue. It is awesome for giving meats, veggies, and fruits a smoky taste. Heat up the grill first and use marinades to make it even tastier.

- **Roasting**: Roasting is cooking food in the oven at higher temperatures. This makes the outside crispy and the inside juicy. It is perfect for meats, veggies and even nuts. You will need a roasting pan, and do not forget to baste meats for more juiciness.

- **Steaming**: Steaming is known as cooking with steam generated by boiling water. We use it to keep the good stuff in veggies, fish, and dumplings. You can use a steamer basket or even a colander to do this.

- **Frying**: Frying is cooking by putting food in hot oil. It gives a crispy texture, such as with fries, chicken, or tempura. Remember to check the oil temperature with a thermometer so things do not burn.

- **Simmering**: Simmering is cooking things slowly at low heat. We do this for soups, stews, and sauces to let the flavors mix. Keep it at a gentle simmer so things do not overcook.

- **Blanching**: Blanching is boiling things quickly and then cooling them down fast. We often do this with vegetables to keep their color and texture. Have some ice water ready to cool things right after boiling.

- **Grating and Mincing**: Grating and mincing are ways to make food into smaller pieces. It is handy for things such as cheese, garlic, or ginger to add flavor to dishes. Just pick the right grater or mincing tool for the size you want.

Household Chores and Organization Tips:

Common household chores vary from washing dishes and doing laundry to vacuuming, sweeping, and keeping shared spaces tidy. A well-maintained living environment gives you a positive atmosphere, reduces stress, and instills a sense of responsibility. When it comes to dividing chores among family members or roommates, communication is extremely important. Having an open discussion about everyone's preferences, strengths, and availability helps distribute tasks fairly. Consider creating a chore chart or schedule (such as the one given below), outlining who is responsible for what on a weekly or monthly basis. When everyone in the household follows a consistent schedule, it fosters a sense of teamwork and shared responsibility.

CHORE CHART

TASK	S	M	T	W	TH	F	S
_____	○	○	○	○	○	○	○
_____	○	○	○	○	○	○	○
_____	○	○	○	○	○	○	○
_____	○	○	○	○	○	○	○
_____	○	○	○	○	○	○	○
_____	○	○	○	○	○	○	○
_____	○	○	○	○	○	○	○
_____	○	○	○	○	○	○	○
_____	○	○	○	○	○	○	○
_____	○	○	○	○	○	○	○
_____	○	○	○	○	○	○	○
_____	○	○	○	○	○	○	○

NOTES

Home Organization and Cleaning:

To keep your living space clean and organized it is necessary to get rid of items that are not in use. The process is known as decluttering, and here is how you can do it:

- **Start Small:** Tackling an entire living space can be overwhelming. Begin with a small area, like a desk or a closet, and gradually expand to larger spaces.

- **Declutter Room after Room:** Focus on one room at a time. This helps prevent feeling overwhelmed and allows you to see tangible progress.

- **Sort all the items**: Divide your belongings into categories such as keep, donate, and discard. Be honest about whether you genuinely need or use each item.

- **Use the Kon Mari Method**: Follow Marie Kondo's method by keeping only items that "spark joy." This approach can help you make more emotionally connected decisions about your possessions.

- **Storage Solutions**: Invest in storage solutions such as bins, baskets, and organizers to keep similar items together. Utilize under-bed storage, wall shelves, and hooks to maximize space.

- **Use Vertical Space:** Install shelves or hooks on walls to make use of vertical space. This is especially beneficial in smaller rooms.

- **Label the Stuff:** Label storage bins and containers to easily identify their contents. This makes finding things and maintaining organization simpler.

- **Declutter Digitally As Well**: Extend your decluttering to digital space. Organize files on your computer, delete unnecessary emails, and declutter your phone by deleting unused apps and organizing the rest.

- **Evaluate Clothing**: When it comes to your wardrobe, consider the one-year rule. If you have not worn an item in the past year, it might be time to donate or discard it.

- **Sentimental Items**: While sentimental items are precious, consider consolidating or displaying them in a way that does not contribute to clutter. Create a special space for sentimental objects rather than scattering them all over your living area.

- **Donate Responsibly**: When donating items, ensure they are in good condition. Many organizations have specific guidelines for accepting donations, so check before dropping off items.

Cleaning Techniques and Schedules

You can also organize your cleaning around a set schedule to maintain much-needed consistency. Here is a simple and basic schedule that divides your cleaning into daily, weekly, and monthly cleaning regimens.

Bedrooms:
Daily:
Make your bed to instantly make the room look neater.
Put away clothes and personal items.
Weekly:
Dust surfaces, including furniture and baseboards.
Vacuum or sweep the floors.
Change the bed linens.
Monthly:
Wipe down light switches, doorknobs, and other frequently touched
Rotate and flip the mattress for even wear.

Kitchen:
Daily:
Wash dishes or load them into the dishwasher.
Wipe down kitchen counters and tables.
Sweep or vacuum the kitchen floor.
Weekly:
Clean out the refrigerator, discarding expired items.
Disinfect kitchen surfaces, including countertops and the sink.
Mop the kitchen floor.
Monthly:
Empty and clean the inside of the microwave.
Check and clean the oven if necessary.
Wipe down cabinet exteriors.

Bathrooms:
Daily:
Wipe down bathroom surfaces, including the sink and countertop.
Squeegee shower doors or wipe down shower walls after use.
Weekly:
Clean the toilet, bathtub and shower.
Change and wash bath mats and towels.
Empty the bathroom trash.
Monthly:
Scrub grout and tiles in the shower or bath.
Clean and disinfect toothbrush holders and soap dispensers.
Check and replace any worn-out shower curtains or liners.

Living Room and Common Areas:
Daily:
Straighten cushions and pillows.
Put away items that are out of place.
Weekly:
Dust surfaces, including furniture and electronics.
Vacuum or clean the floors.
Clean any glass surfaces (e.g., coffee tables, TV screens).
Monthly:
Rotate and fluff cushions to maintain even wear.
Clean upholstery as needed.
Check and clean air vents and filters.

Time Management for Home Maintenance:

I get it! Balancing chores with school, extracurriculars, and social activities is not easy, but we cannot run away from our responsibilities as well. So, employ effective strategies to balance it out and create a schedule that allocates specific times for chores, schoolwork, and personal activities. First, break down tasks into manageable chunks. Time management becomes even more crucial when it comes to home maintenance and cleaning routines. Follow the above schedule to keep it organized. Teamwork and cooperation within the household can make it easier. When family members or roommates work together, chores become less of a burden for everyone. Divide tasks based on individual strengths and preferences to create a sense of shared responsibility.

ACTIVITY 8: COOK A MEAL

It's time to share your cooking skills with your family and friends. Start by cooking something very basic and simple that you like, and then invite your family and friends to eat and share their feedback.

HOME
SURVIVAL

9

CHAPTER 9:

CIVIC ENGAGEMENT AND GLOBAL AWARENESS

While it is important to take care of ourselves as individuals, it is also important to take care of the society we live in. We all need to play our role as responsible citizens and recognize our interconnectedness with the overall fabric of society. From being environmentally conscious to treating others with empathy and actively engaging in community efforts, every choice we make influences the world we live in. It is not just about our individual journey but about how we collectively shape the society we share. So, let's actively play our part, make thoughtful decisions, and work collaboratively to build a community that thrives on understanding, compassion, and shared progress.

Understanding Social Issues and Diversity

Social issues, whether we realize it or not, directly or indirectly impact us and the people we care about. Whether it is issues like inequality, discrimination, or climate change, they weave into our lives in various ways. So, when we take time to understand and raise awareness about these matters, we are not just making the world better for others; we are also creating a more just and healthier environment for ourselves and our loved ones to thrive in.

Exploring Social Issues:

These are the big challenges that impact our community or society, such as unfairness, discrimination, climate change, and mental health struggles. It is extremely important to know what is going on around us. Now, why does it matter to understand different viewpoints and experiences related to these issues? Well, think of it like this: everyone sees the world a bit differently based on their life experiences. So, how do we educate ourselves about these social issues? You do not learn them through textbooks or lectures. Read articles, watch documentaries, and have open conversations with people who have different backgrounds and experiences.

Embrace diversity and inclusion:

Let's think of a world where everyone looked the same, believed the same things, and had the same experiences. It sounds a bit dull, right? Diversity is the secret ingredient that makes our society so vibrant and dynamic. It is not just about appearances; it is about different backgrounds, beliefs, cultures, and perspectives coming together to create a rich tapestry of human experience.

Now, why is it crucial to accept and celebrate diversity? Well, think about a team where each member brings a unique skill or idea to the table. That diversity of talents is what makes the team stronger, more creative, and better equipped to tackle challenges. Similarly, in society, accepting diversity is a superpower. It opens up opportunities for learning from one another, broadens our horizons, and sparks innovation. When we accept and respect one another, it creates a sense of belonging for everyone. It is being part of a big, supportive community where everyone's voice matters. This harmony is the key to building a society where people feel valued, understood, and empowered.

Address social injustice:

Social injustice is when some people are treated unfairly or face obstacles because of things such as their race, gender, or economic status. Now, you might wonder, "How does this relate to me as a teenager?" Well, imagine a friend being treated differently because of who they are; that is not cool, right? Social injustice affects us all by creating an unequal world.

Now, what can you, as a teenager, do about it? First off, educate yourself on these issues. Understand what is happening and why it is extremely important. You do not have to be an expert, but being informed is a great start. Second, use your voice. Share what you learn with friends, on social media, or even in school projects. Your voice can spark conversations and make a difference. Third, get involved in local initiatives or join groups that fight against social injustice. Attend events or discussions to connect with others who care about making things fairer.

Lastly, be an ally. If you see someone being treated unfairly, speak up and show support. It might feel small, but those actions create a ripple effect. By understanding the relevance of social injustice, educating yourself, using your voice, getting involved, and being an ally, you are not just a teenager; you are a force for positive change in the world.

Get Involved in Community Service or Volunteering:

We do not realize it, but we all have the power to make a real difference in our society through community service or volunteering. By doing this, you will be doing good for others and shaping the kind of community you want to live in. Whether it is joining a local clean-up crew, volunteering at an animal shelter, or helping out at a community event, your time and effort can create positive ripples. Through volunteering, you not only lend a hand to those in need but also gain valuable skills, make new friends, and build a sense of responsibility. It is a win-win for all!

Identify the volunteer opportunities:

If you are looking to dive into volunteering, there are tons of cool opportunities for you, such as:

- Community Service Projects: Get involved in local community service initiatives such as clean-up events, tree planting, or neighborhood beautification projects.

- Youth Leadership Programs: Enroll in programs designed for youth leadership development, focusing on honing leadership skills while working on projects that bring positive changes to the community.

" Tutoring and Mentoring: Offer your time as a volunteer tutor or mentor for younger students, providing help with homework, academic subjects, or personal development.

" Animal Shelters: Contribute to local animal shelters by taking care of animals, assisting with adoption events, or supporting various shelter activities.

" Hospitals and Healthcare Facilities: Volunteer your time at hospitals or healthcare facilities, providing support to patients, assisting with administrative tasks, or organizing recreational activities.

" Environmental Conservation: Participate in environmental initiatives such as tree-planting drives, beach clean-ups, or spreading awareness about sustainable practices.

" Homeless Shelters and Food Banks: Assist at homeless shelters or food banks by organizing food drives and helping distribute meals or essential supplies to those in need.

" Elderly Care: Volunteer at senior centers or nursing homes, spending time with elderly residents, organizing activities, or offering companionship.

" Sports Coaching: Volunteer as a sports coach for youth teams or assist in organizing sports events within the community.

" Civic Engagement: Participate in youth councils or engage in local government initiatives where teens can express their opinions and contribute to community decision-making.

" Arts and Culture Programs: Volunteer at local museums, theaters, or cultural events, assisting with organizing exhibits, performances, or workshops.

Benefits of Community Service:

On a personal level, providing community is a powerful way to develop empathy, compassion, and a profound sense of responsibility towards others. Through volunteer work, you gain a deeper understanding of the challenges faced by different segments of society. Plus, the act of giving back contributes greatly to your personal growth and skill development. It provides opportunities to develop communication, teamwork, and problem-solving skills. Beyond personal advantages, community service has a positive ripple effect on society by addressing critical needs, fostering a sense of unity, and building stronger, more interconnected communities.

Sustaining Commitment to Service:

But how will I manage my school and community work? It is a valid concern, and many teens find themselves questioning the feasibility of juggling academic responsibilities with volunteer commitments. The key lies in discovering a harmonious balance. Here is a sample one-week timetable for you to effectively manage community service or volunteering along with studies, school, and extracurricular activities:

Monday:

- 8:00 AM–3:00 PM: School
- 3:30 PM–5:00 PM: Homework and Study Session
- 5:30 PM–7:00 PM: Volleyball Practice
- 7:30 PM–9:00 PM: Dinner and Relaxation

Tuesday:

- 8:00 AM–3:00 PM: School
- 3:30 PM–5:00 PM: Community Service/Volunteering
- 5:30 PM–7:00 PM: Guitar Lessons
- 7:30 PM–9:00 PM: Free Time/Relaxation

Wednesday:

- 8:00 AM–3:00 PM: School
- 3:30 PM–5:00 PM: Homework and Study Session
- 5:30 PM–7:00 PM: Art Club
- 7:30 PM–9:00 PM: Dinner and Relaxation

Thursday:

- 8:00 AM–3:00 PM: School
- 3:30 PM–5:00 PM: Community Service/Volunteering
- 5:30 PM–7:00 PM: Basketball Practice
- 7:30 PM–9:00 PM: Free Time/Relaxation

Friday:

- 8:00 AM–3:00 PM: School
- 3:30 PM–5:00 PM: Homework and Study Session
- 5:30 PM–7:00 PM: Drama Club
- 7:30 PM–9:00 PM: Dinner and Relaxation

Saturday:

- 9:00 AM–11:00 AM: Community Service/Volunteering
- 11:30 AM–2:00 PM: Study Group
- 2:30 PM–5:00 PM: Free Time/Relaxation
- 5:30 PM–7:00 PM: Part-time Job (if applicable)
- 7:30 PM–9:00 PM: Dinner and Social Time

Sunday:

- 10:00 AM–12:00 PM: Family Time
- 12:30 PM–2:00 PM: Free Time/Relaxation
- 2:30 PM–4:00 PM: Personal Project/Passion Pursuit
- 4:30 PM–6:00 PM: Dinner and Relaxation
- 6:30 PM–8:00 PM: Movie or Reading Time

Remember, flexibility is key, so you can adjust this timetable based on your specific needs and commitments.

Developing a Sense of Global Citizenship:

In today's interconnected world, being aware of what is happening globally is not just an academic exercise; it is a life skill. It helps you develop critical thinking, empathy, and a sense of responsibility. Plus, it equips you to thrive in a diverse and dynamic society.

Understanding Global Issues:

"The more youth begin to recognize that they have a voice, the more change is possible."
— Usher

So, yes! Even though you are young and growing, your voices do matter. There are a wide variety of issues that you must learn about and raise awareness about to let the world know what you stand for. Some key issues that you must learn about are climate change, environmental degradation, poverty, inequality, access to education, healthcare disparities, human rights violations, political instability, and the ongoing challenges posed by global health crises.

Firstly, use digital platforms and reputable news sources to get up-to-date information on ongoing crisises. Follow international news outlets, subscribe to reliable newsletters, and utilize social media responsibly to get a continuous stream of global updates. You can engage in discussions, participate in global awareness programs and join online forums to gain diverse perspectives and create a sense of interconnectedness. You can participate in "Model United Nations" programs, in your country to understand how international policymaking works and learn about the workings of international collaborations. You can create your own discussion panel with friends to share your views to opinions regarding rising global issues to apprise each other of the latest developments.

Educational initiatives, such as incorporating global perspectives into school curricula or participating in international exchange programs, can provide firsthand experiences and insights. Plus, involvement in youth-led organizations focused on global issues, attending conferences, and engaging in community service with an international focus are effective ways for teens to actively contribute to addressing global challenges.

Taking Action for Global Causes:

The power of action lies in your hands, as you are the future of this world! Your understanding of today's issues can help you make better choices in the coming years. As responsible global citizens, you play a vital role in addressing issues such as poverty, climate change, and inequality.

Join or support international NGOs, participate in global awareness campaigns, and explore virtual or in-person volunteer opportunities with a global focus. You can also collaborate with your schools, local organizations, or youth groups to organize fundraisers or events that raise awareness and support for global causes.

Advocate for global issues like those of young climate activist Greta Thunberg and education activist Malala, and raise awareness in your communities through effective communication and collaboration. Malala Yousuf Zai was only 15 years old when she took a bullet by extremists while advocating for girl's education. But she did not stop there and continued to do so, and today she is running various schools in all parts of the world to provide free-of-cost education to young girls. That is the power of a teenage mindset. You all are capable of doing wonders; you just have to feel it in yourself and step up!

If you do not have the resources you can raise your voice on social media platforms, create and share educational content, organize community events, and collaborate with local organizations to amplify global issues. Engaging in open conversations, sharing personal experiences, and utilizeing creative mediums, such as art or storytelling, can effectively convey the importance of global awareness to a broader audience.

In short, as a teen, you have the ability to cultivate a mindset that embraces the world beyond your immediate surroundings. By staying informed, using technology, supporting global causes, practicing empathy, and engaging in meaningful conversations, you contribute to creating a more interconnected and compassionate world around you.

ACTIVITY 9: CREATE A PRESENTATION

Is there any global issue that is close to your heart? Such as climate change, poverty, human trafficking, etc. Then do research on that topic and create a short presentation or social media post to raise awareness about it among your friends and classmates.

GLOBAL HEARTS, LOCAL HANDS

10

CHAPTER 10:

RISE AND BOUNCE BACK: SUPER SKILLS FOR TOUGH TIMES

"Success is not final; failure is not fatal; it is the courage to continue that count."
- Winston Churchill

Tough times are like a bumpy road. The super skill you need to deal with them is the ability to bounce back like a rubber ball. You know what they say: "When the going gets tough, the tough get going." It means that when things get hard, remember that it is not the end; setbacks are detours, and you can fight back harder to rise above them. You have the power to get back up, keep going, and become even better.

Bounce Back from Tough Times:

Say you have been working hard on a big school project for weeks. The presentation day arrives, and things do not go as you planned. Your slides are mixed up, and you stumble over your words. It feels like a total flop, and you are embarrassed. But here is the bounce-back moment: instead of letting it ruin your day, you take a deep breath, crack a joke about the mix-up, and continue with confidence. You show everyone that mistakes happen, but they do not define who you are. Later, you go back, fix the slides, and decide to use this experience as a chance to learn how to handle unexpected situations better next time. This is what bouncing back does to you; it turns failure into success. You cannot avoid failures in life; what you can do is learn to stand back up again when you fall down.

Understanding Resilience:

*"Resilience is the antidote to complacency.
It's the mindset that allows you to push
beyond your limits and achieve
greatness."*
– David Goggins

Do you know what resilience is? Through resilience, you cultivate inner strength to confront challenges, setbacks, and unexpected changes. Rather than avoiding difficulties, resilience enables you to confront them with bravery and flexibility. Especially in times of hardship, resilience becomes crucial as it equips you with the capacity to navigate through tough situations, extract valuable lessons from experiences, and emerge more robust. Here are some strategies to help you develop resilience:

- Positive Mindset: Create a positive outlook by focusing on what you can control. Look for the silver lining in difficult situations.

- Self-reflection: Take time to reflect on your experiences. Understand your emotions and thoughts, and learn from both successes and setbacks.

- Social Support: Build a strong support network with friends, family, or mentors. Sharing your feelings and seeking advice can provide valuable perspectives.

- Problem-solving skills: Develop effective problem-solving skills. Break down challenges into smaller, manageable steps and tackle them one at a time.

- Adaptability: Life is full of surprises, and being flexible can help you navigate unexpected situations.

- Healthy Lifestyle: Prioritize physical health through regular exercise, proper nutrition, and sufficient sleep. A healthy body contributes to a resilient mind.

- Mindfulness and Relaxation Techniques: Practice mindfulness, meditation, or deep-breathing exercises. These techniques can help you manage stress and stay grounded.

- Learn from Failures: View failures as opportunities to learn and grow. Understand that setbacks are a natural part of life's journey.

- Set Realistic Goals: Set achievable goals that align with your abilities and circumstances. Celebrate small victories and progress along the way.

- Crisis Planning: Have a crisis plan in place for particularly challenging situations. Knowing how to respond can provide a sense of control.

- Develop a Sense of Purpose: Have a sense of purpose by engaging in activities that bring you joy and fulfillment. Having a purpose can fuel your resilience.

Coping Strategies for Tough Times:

Picture yourself as a smartphone, just as your mobile phone needs regular charging and updates to function at its best. Similarly, you need self-care to give yourself the necessary recharge. You need to take time for activities that bring you joy, relaxation, and a sense of well-being. Whether it is talking to friends, going for a run, or practicing mindfulness, these coping strategies keep your mental and emotional well-being in check. So, just like you would not ignore your phone's needs, do not neglect yours either. Try these simple yet powerful methods to rejuvenate your mind and recharge your energy level:

- Gratitude Practice: Reflect on things you are grateful for each day. This practice shifts your focus toward positive aspects of your life.

- Focus on Solutions: Instead of dwelling on problems, channel your energy into finding solutions. This proactive approach can empower you.

- Be with Positivity: Engage with positive influences, whether it is uplifting music, inspirational quotes, or supportive friends. Create an environment that fosters optimism.

- Learn from Challenges: View challenges as opportunities for growth. Each difficulty presents a chance to learn, adapt, and become more resilient.

- Visualize: Let's think of a positive outcome in challenging situations. Visualization can create a mental image of success and reinforce optimism.

- Stay Present: Focus on the present moment rather than worrying about the future. Mindfulness techniques, such as deep breathing, ттcan help keep you grounded.

- Celebrate Small Wins: Acknowledge and celebrate even the smallest achievements. This builds positive momentum and a sense of accomplishment.

- Practice self-compassion: Treat yourself with kindness during tough times. Understand that everyone faces challenges, and it is okay not to be perfect.

- Be with your support system: Look for support from friends, family, or mentors. Positive social connections can provide encouragement and perspective.

- Set realistic goals: Break larger goals into smaller, achievable steps. Meeting these milestones boosts confidence and reinforces a positive mindset.

- Limit Negative Influences: Minimize exposure to negative news or people who bring you down. Be positive to nurture optimism.

Learn from Your Adversity:

Tough times, while challenging, can serve as profound opportunities for your personal growth and learning. When you face difficulties, you are being handed a puzzle; each piece represents a chance to understand yourself better and develop valuable life skills.

Reflecting on experiences during challenging situations is key. By asking yourself what you have learned and how you have grown, you uncover valuable lessons that contribute to your resilience.

Turn Your Fails into Wins:

Failure is not the end but a pivotal moment, a crossroads where one can choose to be defeated or rise above the circumstances. It is a teacher disguised in disappointment who offers you profound lessons for those willing to learn. Every failed attempt is a brushstroke on the canvas of experience, shaping individuals into resilient beings capable of enduring life's challenges.

See Your Failure as A Learning Opportunity:

The first step in turning fails into wins is accepting failure as a natural part of the journey. Instead of viewing it as a dead end, consider it a detour, an unexpected route that might lead to unexplored opportunities. Take the time to understand what went wrong. List the reasons and work on them. Failure, when viewed through the lens of growth becomes a catalyst of change rather than a death sentence. It propels you to set higher goals, hone you skills and strive for excellence. Each misstep is an invitation to recalibrate, refine strategies and approach challenges with newfound wisdom.

Take example of Michael Jordan– the greatest basketball player of all time. Do you know that Jordan was initially cut from his own school's varsity basketball team. That was the first failure that fueled his success. He did not back down and kept practicing and excelling until he became the greatest of all times. He not only made the team the following year but also earned a scholarship to the University of North Carolina. He faced more challenges in the NBA, such as early playoff exits and criticism for not winning championships. However, Jordan used these setbacks as motivation to work harder and elevate his game. That is the power of resilience! It is a force that keeps you going.

Developing a Growth Mindset:

What Michael Jordan, Steve Jobs, and all other successful names in the world have in common is a "growing mindset." It is your mindset that tells you that your abilities and intelligence can grow with effort, learning, and perseverance. It does not let you sit and accept what life throws at you. It pushes you to achieve the unimaginable. This mindset is a game-changer because it means you are not stuck with a fixed set of skills; you can always get better at anything with practice and determination. The growth mindset is not something we are born with, but something we develop. When we learn to break the apparent chains of limitations, we develop a growth mindset. Here is how you can make that possible for you as well!

- " Learn from your criticism. Instead of feeling down when someone gives feedback, see it as a chance to get better.

- " Keep putting in your effort. Understand that putting in effort is what leads to improvement.

- " Persist in the face of setbacks. Do not give up easily. Let's say you are trying to unlock a new level and even if you fail a few times, keep going until you succeed.

- " Get inspired by others. Look at successful people as inspiration, not as competition.

- " Celebrate Others' Success: When your friends succeed, be happy for them.

- " Love Learning: Enjoy the process of learning itself.

Adapt and evolve from setbacks:

Jann Mardenborough is a compelling example when it comes to showcasing the power of determination and pursuing one's passion. Initially aspiring to become a professional football player, Jann's life took an unexpected turn when he entered the Nissan GT Academy competition, a virtual-to-reality racing competition that aimed to turn video gamers into real-life race car drivers. Despite having no prior experience in motorsports, Jann emerged as the winner of the competition in 2011.

His transition from a gamer to a professional racing driver was met with skepticism, but Jann remained steadfast in his determination to succeed in the world of motorsports. Through rigorous training, hard work, and a commitment to continuously improve his skills, he climbed the ranks of competitive racing. Jann's story highlights the transformative potential of perseverance and adapting to unexpected opportunities.

Determination is the inner fire that fuels your journey. It is making a decision to stick with your goal, even when Netflix and social media are tempting you to stray. Determination is that voice inside saying, "I have got this, and I won't give up." So, when life throws tough levels your way, remember your superpowers—persistence, the ability to keep going, determination, the decision to stick with it. Together, they make you an unstoppable force, ready to tackle anything that comes your way

Develop problem-solving and adaptability Skills:

Problem-solving is your ability to fight the challenges and find creative solutions. Adaptability is your skill of adjusting to changes and rebounding from setbacks. Together, these skills help you steer through unexpected plot twists in a story, changing strategies while still coming out on top. Problem-solving is a skill that improves with practice. The more you face challenges and work through them, the more confident and effective you will become at solving problems in various aspects of your life.

First, identify the problem: Clearly understand what the issue is. Sometimes, it helps to write it down to get a better grasp.

Brainstorm multiple solutions: Come up with as many possible solutions as you can. Do not worry about evaluating them at this stage; just get your ideas out.

Evaluate practical solutions: Consider the pros and cons of each solution. Think about the potential consequences and how well each option aligns with your goals.

Choose the perfect solution. Pick the solution that seems the most practical and effective. Trust your instincts, but also consider the information you have gathered during the evaluation step.

Implement the solution: Put your chosen solution into action. This may involve specific steps or changes in your behavior or environment.

Evaluate your results. After implementing the solution, assess how well it worked. Did it solve the problem, or do you need to adjust your approach?

Techniques for Effective Problem Solving:

- **Critical Thinking:** Be a logical thinker. Analyze information, question assumptions, and consider different perspectives.

- **Creativity:** Think outside the box. Do not be afraid to come up with unique and innovative solutions.

- **Communication:** Talk to others about your problem. They might offer valuable insights or suggestions you have not thought of.

- **Time Management:** Break the problem-solving process into manageable steps and allocate time to each. This prevents feeling overwhelmed.

- **Positive Attitude:** Approach problems with a positive mindset. See challenges as opportunities to learn and grow.

- **Resilience:** Understand that not every solution works perfectly. Learn from failures, adjust your approach, and try again.

Building adaptability and flexibility:

Let's say you are playing a video game where the levels keep changing and you have to adapt quickly to new challenges. One day, your favorite character faces a surprise attack, the game world transforms and you will have to change your usual strategies This is where adaptability comes in: instead of getting frustrated, you quickly learn to use new weapons, discover hidden paths, and even team up with other characters to overcome obstacles. Similarly, in real life, you need to be adaptable to handle unexpected changes, whether it is a sudden change in school plans, a new responsibility, or unexpected events. It is the key to mastering the dynamic levels of life's game! The way to stay flexible and adaptable is to keep your mind open to change.

They say that "change is the only constant in life", which means that nothing is meant to stay static and the same. The earlier you accept this fact, the easier it will become for you to not only embrace the change but also to change your plans and strategies according to it. What if you do not get admission to your favorite college? Would you give up? No! You try to get into the second-best college and focus on your educational career to make the most of it. Flexibility eases your life, and you roll with the changing winds. The more rigid a person becomes, the greater the chance of life-breaking or shattering his dream. Be like a flowing stream of water that carves its way to its destination through the sturdiest rocks only through consistent and directional efforts.

ACTIVITY 10: RESILIENCE JOURNAL

Create a resilience journal. Recall your recent setbacks or challenges and write down your thoughts on how you are working to overcome them. Add positive affirmations or quotes to inspire resilience.

RISE ON WHEELS

CONCLUSION

Hey, my young readers! As we have reached the end of this book, I would like to congratulate you on successfully going through all the chapters. The teenage years are indeed filled with challenges and discoveries, and your decision to actively look for resources for growth speaks volumes about your commitment to self-improvement. So, celebrate your journey and pledge to make positive changes in the future!

In this book, we have looked into various challenges of teenage life and how to overcome them, starting from addressing self-esteem issues and navigating relationships to managing academic expectations, peer pressures, money problems, health challenges, and the quest for self-discovery. Perhaps we have covered a spectrum of challenges that resonate with your unique experiences. I hope that you have learned a great deal from this book and will practically implement all the shared strategies in your life to harness their benefits.

As you close this book and move forward, keep in mind that learning life skills is an ongoing process. This book is just the beginning of your journey. Every challenge you face, every mistake you make, and every failure you come across is a stepping stone towards becoming the person you aspire to become. You are not alone in this process. Always reach out for support from your family, friends, teachers, counsellors, and professionals. Look for knowledge and continue to explore the vast potential within you. This teenage maze may seem complex right now, but with the set of skills and insights you have gained from this book, I am confident you will power through it with resilience, wisdom, and a sense of purpose.

Here is to your continued success on the amazing journey that lies ahead of you all!

REFERENCES

Anderson, K., & Hq, W. (2019). *Who is Michael Jordan? Penguin.*

Buhle, J. T., Silvers, J. A., Wager, T. D., Lopez, R. B., Onyemekwu, C., Kober, H., Weber, J., & Ochsner, K. N. (2013). Cognitive Reappraisal of Emotion: A Meta-Analysis of Human Neuroimaging Studies. *Cerebral Cortex, 24(11)*, 2981–2990. https://doi.org/10.1093/cercor/bht154

Campbell, D. J. (2019). *The 24 hour rule: Determining Your Dating Partner's Marriage Potential in 30 Days.* Independently Published.

Cirillo, F. (2018). *The Pomodoro technique: The Acclaimed Time-Management System That Has Transformed How We Work.* Currency.

Conzemius, A., & O'Neill, J. (2009). *The power of SMART goals: Using Goals to Improve Student Learning.* Solution Tree Press.

Giant, N. (2019). *Life skills and career coaching for teens: A Practical Manual for Supporting School Engagement, Aspirations and Success in Young People aged 11–18.* Jessica Kingsley Publishers.

Isaacson, W. (2011). *Steve Jobs.* Simon and Schuster.

McGee, E. (2020). *How to be good with money.* Gill & Macmillan Ltd.

McPherson, F. (2018). *Mnemonics for Study (2nd ed.).* Wayz Press.

Mecham, J. (2017). *You need a budget: The Proven System for Breaking the Paycheck-to-Paycheck Cycle, Getting Out of Debt, and Living the Life You Want.* HarperCollins.

Ramsey, D. (2009). *The total money makeover: A Proven Plan for Financial Fitness.* Thomas Nelson Inc.

Ramsey, D., & Cruze, R. (2014). *Smart money smart kids: Raising the Next Generation to Win with Money.* Ramsey Press.

Reads, S. (2020). *Insights on Francesco Cirillo's the Pomodoro Technique.* Swift Books LLC.

Records, G. W. (2014). *Guinness World Records Gamer's Edition 2015 ebook.* Guinness World Records.

Rowell, R. (2014). *Malala Yousafzai: education activist*. ABDO.

Seligman, M. E. P., Steen, T. A., Park, N., & Peterson, C. (2005). Positive Psychology Progress: Empirical Validation of Interventions. *American Psychologist*, *60*(5), 410–421. https://doi.org/10.1037/0003-066x.60.5.410

Sethi, R. (2010). *I will teach you to be rich: No guilt, no excuses - just a 6-week programme that works*. Hachette UK.

Sin, N. L., & Lyubomirsky, S. (2009). Enhancing well-being and alleviating depressive symptoms with positive psychology interventions: a practice-friendly meta-analysis. *Journal of Clinical Psychology*, *65*(5), 467–487. https://doi.org/10.1002/jclp.20593

Tracy, B. (2008). *Eat that frog!: 21 Great Ways to Stop Procrastinating and Get More Done in Less Time*. ReadHowYouWant.com.

Tracy, B. (2013). *Motivation (The Brian Tracy Success Library)*. AMACOM.

Wolff, A. (2014). *Khan Academy and Salman Khan*. The Rosen Publishing Group, Inc.

Images retrieved from Canva.com

Made in the USA
Las Vegas, NV
09 April 2024

88450177R00118